*A CORD OF THR[EE]
STRANDS IS N[OT]
QUICKLY BROKEN.*

ECCLESIASTES 4:12

PRAISE FOR
BECOMING YOUR FAVORITE CHURCH

Becoming Your Favorite Church is a powerful and
valuable antidote to ministry frustrations and error.
It should be read by lay leaders and pastors alike.
The phenomenal wisdom and experience of Drs. London
and Wiseman make almost every page of this book
a treasure to be cherished.

BISHOP CHARLES E. BLAKE, SR.
MINISTER, WEST ANGELES CHURCH OF GOD IN CHRIST
LOS ANGELES, CALIFORNIA

Christian worship centers need, above all else, competent
leadership. For the legions of Christ's followers who march to the
drumbeat of church life, these capable authors have provided a most
helpful measuring device—a kind of calibrated scale by which to
evaluate and, if necessary, to change one's ministry.

HOWARD G. HENDRICKS
DISTINGUISHED PROFESSOR AND CHAIRMAN
CENTER FOR CHRISTIAN LEADERSHIP
DALLAS THEOLOGICAL SEMINARY

This volume is incredibly pertinent and wonderfully helpful.
I have been a pastor for many years and wish that the things
written in this volume had been in my head, hands and heart much,
much earlier. I am happy to commend it.

ADRIAN ROGERS

SENIOR PASTOR, BELLEVUE BAPTIST CHURCH
MEMPHIS, TENNESSEE

Find a pastor who doesn't have one hand on the exit door!
This book shows how to remove that hand and free it for transforming
ministry. The section on 49 ways to affirm your pastor is the ideal commentary on 1 Thessalonians 5:12-13 (appreciate your pastors
highly in love) and alone is worth the price of the book.

LEONARD SWEET

DREW THEOLOGICAL SCHOOL AND
GEORGE FOX EVANGELICAL SEMINARY

BECOMING YOUR
FAVORITE
CHURCH

H. B. LONDON, JR.
NEIL B. WISEMAN

Regal

From Gospel Light
Ventura, California, U.S.A.

Published by Regal Books
From Gospel Light
Ventura, California, U.S.A.
Printed in the U.S.A.

Cover and interior design by Robert Williams
Revised edition edited by Steven Lawson

Library of Congress Cataloging-in-Publication Data
London, H. B.
    Becoming your favorite church / H. B. London and Neil B. Wiseman.
        p. cm.
    Includes bibliographical references.
    ISBN 0-8307-2904-6
    1. Christian leadership. 2. Group ministry. I. Wiseman, Neil B. II. Title.
    BV652.1 .L65 2002
    253—dc21   2001008731

1 2 3 4 5 6 7 8 9 10 11 12 13 14 15 / 09 08 07 06 05 04 03 02

Rights for publishing this book in other languages are contracted by Gospel Light Worldwide, the international nonprofit ministry of Gospel Light. Gospel Light Worldwide also provides publishing and technical assistance to international publishers dedicated to producing Sunday School and Vacation Bible School curricula and books in the languages of the world. For additional information, visit www.gospellightworldwide.org; write to Gospel Light Worldwide, P.O. Box 3875, Ventura, CA 93006; or send an e-mail to info@gospellightworldwide.org.

CONTENTS

FOREWORD

Becoming Your Favorite Church—what a unique title for an insightful book! Every page stretches lay leaders and ministers to become more and more like Christ and offers guidance for Holy Spirit-inspired teamwork between laypersons and pastors to make churches healthy and robust for God. In almost prophetic ways this book reminds us that the Church is you, not somebody else. It is us, not "them." It is we, not "those folks."

This message calls church leaders to the soul-growing experience of giving up being corporate board members who make decisions at church to becoming a team of twenty-first-century disciples in partnership with the living Christ. The goal is to do His work in the church, the community and the world.

Becoming Your Favorite Church takes us back to Jesus' original plan, as voiced through the apostle Peter: "You are a chosen people, a royal priesthood, a holy nation, a people belonging to God, that you may declare the praises of him who called you out of darkness into his wonderful light" (1 Pet. 2:9, *NIV*). Note the apostle's powerful use of the word "you." Your favorite church and the desires of "Him who called you . . . into his wonderful light" must be part of the same dream. Being leaders in the Church gives us an opportunity to develop into great Christians, even as we lead.

H. B. London and Neil Wiseman have spoken, written and given years of ministry to refocusing the Church by renewing her pastors. Their books have been read and are being lived out by thousands of pastors around the world. Now they challenge laity to become great

Christians who join Christ-focused ministers to make the Church invincible in our time.

Reading this book could change your life and help make you a Christ-motivated leader whom the Lord can use for spiritual revolution in our time.

Thanks, H. B. and Neil, for another winner!

Dale E. Galloway
Dean, Beeson International
Center for Biblical Preaching
and Church Leadership

AN AFFIRMING WORD TO OUR READERS

Becoming Your Favorite Church—these four words dare every Christian to dream God's dream for His Church and then to commit their hearts and souls to make that dream come true. This book describes what the Church can do and be when pastors and lay leaders work together as one. It is for every person who loves the Church—especially congregational leaders. Precisely, this book is about lay leaders coming alongside pastors to form an effective team.

Scripture uses group word pictures such as "body" and "family" to teach how much a church relies on the combined strengths of congregates. A contemporary example of this same idea is an athletic team.

With the use of sports analogies, this book challenges every Christian to move from spectator status to become a team player on the field. It calls upon each believer to do his or her part to make the church better, stronger and healthier.

The apostle Paul uses the image of the Body of Christ to describe how important it is that the followers of Christ become part of the exciting process of their churches' becoming what they want them to be. He says, "The way God designed our bodies is a model for understanding our lives together as a church: every part dependent on every other part. . . . If one part flourishes, every other part enters into the exuberance. You are Christ's body—that's who you are!" (1 Cor. 12:25-27, *THE MESSAGE*).

Here is what the title *Becoming Your Favorite Church* means:

"Becoming," a hope-filled, inspiring word, underscores the potential God has given for progress and achievement to every church. This can be compared to the potential of a tiny acorn to become a huge oak tree.

"Favorite Church" shouts with the idea of the kind of church you would like your church to become: a haven of hope, a company of the committed, a hospital for sinners, a school for seekers and so much more. Also, a pastor will be drawn by the title because he obviously wants to have a church that is a favorite in everyone's heart.

"Your" underscores the personal relationships you have in your local church. In spite of its faults, your church represents a sanctuary of purpose and a branch of the family of God, a place where people can receive something they cannot find in the world.

Do you want your church to be a favorite among seekers, newcomers and members? If so, then the becoming has begun.

ACKNOWLEDGMENTS

Thanks, colleagues and partners—we love you.

Becoming Your Favorite Church, much more than a book about ministry theories developed in some idyllic detachment from real life, speaks to present-day ministry issues happening at the front lines. These are good days for the Church of Jesus Christ, if we know what to do with them.

These concepts, convictions and heart concerns are lessons learned from wonderful people we served as pastors. Likewise, many other faithful lay leaders outside the congregations we served have sharpened our thoughts.

But there are other even more unique influences that have shaped this book. For reasons known only to God, He took us out of local church pastorates and made us advocates for pastors. In this helping-advocacy role, like a physician learns intricacies about medicine from patients, we have learned from those we serve. That learning that has shaped our ministry every day has come during hundreds of lay retreats and pastors' conferences, preaching assignments in local congregations, guest lecturing in seminary and Bible college chapels and classrooms, mission trips and personal conversations after our presentations, and by phone calls, letters and e-mail messages. Hundreds of you have taught us so much, and we are grateful.

We began writing books together in 1992. Now, a decade later, we are still at it.

When we acknowledge the people who have contributed to writing a book, there is always a danger of forgetting someone. We are hopeful that this will not be the case here.

Our wives, Bonnie and Beverley, have stood faithfully by our sides. Sue McFadden (H. B.'s assistant for nearly 30 years) and Bonnie have improved the words as we put them on paper. Without the assistance of these three talented ladies, our task would have been impossible.

At Focus on the Family, I (H. B.) have been surrounded by faithful colleagues who serve with me in the pastoral ministries department. Dan Davidson, Roger Charman, Eldon Fry, Alex Person and Ralph Kelly have been invaluable in contributing a constant stream of information relating to the local church in America.

Of course, in all of our work, it is the pastors of America and around the world whom we salute, affirm and honor. We are blessed to be partners with the laity of the churches who come alongside them in their ministry. Pastors are our heroes. We believe in what they do and what they can do to renew the Church and change the world. And it is with that astounding potential in mind that this book challenges laity and pastors to work together to change the world for Christ. Thank you, colleagues, both clergy and laypeople.

Special thanks go to the Regal publishing team of Bill Greig III, Kyle Duncan, Kim Bangs and especially to our editor, Steven Lawson. You are tops, and we are grateful for the way you have opened the publishing door to get our message out to contemporary church leaders.

Lastly, we thank you, our readers, who have blessed us by allowing us to step into your lives for a little while. Our prayer for you and the people you serve continues to be for renewal, peace and unity within the Church of Jesus Christ. Go for it!

Neil and H. B.

THE LOCAL CHURCH: GROUND ZERO FOR CHRIST'S MINISTRY

We love the Church. We were born into it, nurtured by it, transformed by its messengers, loved and supported by its people, called into ministry through its Christ-centered message and have found fulfillment in a lifetime of service to it.

At times we struggle with what we see in the Church—at least in our homeland, the United States. It has become somewhat gimmicky, even sadly predictable in its shallowness. Far too much emphasis has been placed on the size of the local church and not nearly enough on the health of the Body. The contemporary Church has tended to make selfless heroes of the Church's superstars and failed to give adequate value and honor to the majority of those who serve in small- to medium-sized congregations. It appears we have softened our approach to the gospel by failing to speak out against sin in fear of being rejected by the very world we are seeking to save. And far too many laity have moved from the action in the arena to a shady spot in the bleachers.

Regardless of how we feel, the Church is God's divine instrument. The gates of hell will not prevail against it (see Matt. 16:18), nor is revival likely to come through any other channel. In so many ways, the Church is the mind of Christ to a confused world.

From time to time, such as after the Columbine High School shootings and the New York twin towers terrorist attack, we see the Church at its best. At such times, the churches we lead and serve represent God's heart, hands and feet and we are able to do His work in the world.

The Church is at its best when the actions of those in its pews mirror the love of Christ rather than the self-centeredness of the world. It is when the Church shares the message of hope and new beginnings and cultivates the personal faith of its people that the true nature of the Body of Christ becomes a force of righteousness in the world.

The Church that Christ created was unified because its members loved its founder and one another as He admonished them to do. They matured into a mighty force as they settled on sound doctrinal practices. They put their differences aside and became generous with one another. Before long, a watching world began to ask, "Why are these people so unique?" The answer was clear: They were amazingly authentic reflections of their leader, Jesus Christ. Look at how they loved one another. When they had conflicts, they worked them out. Mostly they solved their problems by praying together and forgiving one another. We believe that approach to solving problems can work today.

Members of the first Christian community were challenged by a cause that was much greater than the strength and intellect they possessed, but when surrendered to that cause in Jesus' name, they became extravagantly bold and supernaturally successful. We believe that same success is possible in our day and in our churches.

The truth is, today all of us stand on the shoulders of the Church's pioneers, who have always passed the baton of leadership from one generation to another. The next pass promises to be as significant as any has been in the 2,000-year history of the Church. Why? Because in some ways the Church has become marginalized. We seem to have lost our appeal because we have chosen to compromise our message. The marketplace now operates virtually without us—the evangelistic fervor for transforming lives and impacting society that once pulsated in our hearts has been quieted by the roar of an unrighteous and antagonistic world.

We need to rekindle a spark in our individual lives and in our churches by recognizing our God-ordained place in His scheme. We must step up to the challenge, recognize our potential and make a difference.

As the authors of this book, we know that we do not have all the answers, but we are bold enough to share with you some of our thoughts for revitalizing your churches and for rethinking your commitments to the long-running dream Christ has for His Church. There will either be those who stand on your shoulders, who follow your lead, or there will be a void that might never be filled. You can either cling to the baton or eagerly pass it on.

The lines in the sand are pretty well drawn. On one side, the world goes about its own business, scarcely aware of our existence unless there is a need for our services. On the other, the Bride of Christ prepares herself for her greatest challenge: to win over a seemingly disinterested world. Are you ready? If not, what will it take to convince you that you are a mighty force in the hands of a loving but impatient God who is eager to see His gospel make a difference in individual lives and in society?

Our prayer is that you will allow us the privilege of provoking, prodding and stimulating your concepts about the kingdom of God and challenging your resolve with some ideas and strategies that might be worth your prayerful consideration. Some of these ideas might even revolutionize your whole life as a Christian. We hope so.

*The goal of ministry teams is to meet needs
in order to more effectively carry out Christ's mission
in the world. . . . The focus is on serving others
rather than increasing the bottom line.*

C. GENE WILKES, *JESUS ON LEADERSHIP*

CHAPTER 1

LESSONS FROM THE NFL

NEW WAYS TO DEVELOP AN ACHIEVING TEAM

Owner of the Church,
Give our leadership team perspective.
Guide our leadership team to truth.
Enable our leadership team to achieve.
Save us from meaningless activity and empty talk.
Amen.

Jesus developed His disciples into a highly effective force for righteousness that changed the world forever. Shaping fishermen, tax collectors and shepherds into team players must have been tough, frustrating work, even for our Lord. From Jesus' first calls for the disciples to join Him until the last frightening good-byes on the Mount of Transfiguration, He used the events and time they shared together to build these men into a leadership team for the Early Church. As a result, amazingly all but Judas became productive servants in fulfilling the mission of Christ.

What incredible on-the-job training!

Each day Jesus put His disciples through strenuous spiritual workouts, teaching them teamwork. Their conditioning took place in a mobile training camp. Their classrooms included hillsides, roadways and seashores—

once they were in a boat in the middle of a lake! They learned at weddings, funerals and sometimes around tables at mealtime. Jesus frequently used the Old Testament as their playbook. To get them in shape, our Lord drilled them on the fundamentals of love, forgiveness, transformation, dependence on God and holy living. He stretched their stamina almost to the limit when He took them to Gethsemane, Golgotha and the empty tomb.

Jesus' goal was for His team to win something much more significant than a Super Bowl championship, an NCAA title or a World Cup trophy. He wanted them to win their world, a goal that required them to be in top shape spiritually. To get them ready for their incredible conquest, Jesus kindled a team spirit inside them that would not quit, even when they fumbled the ball, double dribbled or missed the shot.

Jesus, the greatest coach of all time, drafted ordinary people, developed them beyond their fondest dreams and produced some of the most effective leaders the Church has ever known. He challenged them to develop their brains, brawn and drive to serve the greatest cause on Earth—a challenge He still offers to disciples today.

To see how the Master Coach, Jesus, transformed His disciples into an invincible force for righteousness inspires all believers. It has in past generations and still does. His model challenges us to be better members of the Jesus team and to build effective leadership teams in our churches. So much of what our Lord built into the first team needs to be replicated in the church leadership teams of today. And it can be!

THE ENORMOUS POTENTIAL OF CHURCH LEADERSHIP TEAMS

Would you describe the working relationships in your church as ultimate examples of teamwork? Are members of your governing

group spectators or servants? Are decision makers active partners who come alongside the pastor to help create a vision and
vitally live out the gospel near trenches of need? Does every
member see the need to be involved in a meaningful way? Is the
solidarity of everyone on the team doing something for Christ
obvious to visitors and new members?

*Wherever Jesus' team model for doing His work
and building His Church has been tried, the people
of God have achieved amazing results.*

Wherever Jesus' team model for doing His work and building His Church has been tried, the people of God have achieved
amazing results. In every generation, disciples increase their
impact on the world when they stop watching from the sidelines
and actually go onto the field to participate in the action. When
team members leave the stands and move onto the playing field,
they automatically create positive peer pressure that keeps them
and others at the task. When they put down their scorecards and
put on their uniforms, they move into position to reach Jesus'
exciting goals for the Church.

When spectators become players, two significant things
happen. As active players, they grow in Christlikeness. The exercise and discipline strengthen their spiritual stamina. Then, at
church they create values, vision and success through their
teamwork.

THE ETERNAL IMPORTANCE OF TEAMWORK

When weighing the significance of teamwork in your church, please consider George Barna's well-documented research: "Churches that use lay leadership teams are more likely to experience a broader base of changed lives as a result of the church's ministry."[1]

To be certain that the implications of his findings are fully understood, Barna goes on to declare: "The bottom line in ministry is whether people accept Jesus Christ as their Savior, and how devoted they are to becoming more Christlike. Lay leadership teams facilitate such commitments and the resulting life change because the church becomes more ministry minded, but less dependent upon the pastor."[2]

Do not miss Barna's basic message to Christian leaders: Great teamwork increases the effectiveness of our evangelism and discipleship. When applying this principle, it is a given that lay leaders will be both women and men, according to the prophecy of Joel 2:28-29, which is confirmed in Acts 2:17-18.

Introducing the team concept of ministry and getting an established church to change may be difficult or misunderstood at first, but so are most things that count.

Too many congregations have assumed or even been taught that the pastor is responsible for every facet of a church's ministry. Working under these expectations, if the church flounders, who gets blamed? The pastor, of course! Even on the best ministry team, the buck ultimately stops with the pastor. But far too often, the minister's effectiveness is cut short simply because the team has not functioned the way it should or a team does not even exist.

TEAM SPORTS AS A MODEL

Let's use a National Football League analogy to develop brand-new perspectives and vigorous strategies for our churches. We have selected this male-dominated sport because we are familiar with it, but the same lessons can be drawn from other professional leagues, including the Women's National Basketball Association.

Recognize the Owner

Every team must have an owner—someone who has paid a hefty price for the franchise. In the NFL and WNBA models, the owner delegates authority to administrators, coaches and some players. But in every decision, the owner always has the right to have the last word.

How does this apply to Christians? We must remember that God owns the Church. It does not belong to the denomination, the pastor or the board. It does not belong to the people who control what they are supposed to serve. Mark it down, make it clear, repeat it often: *God owns the Church.* Just as the owner of a professional sports franchise has the final say, so God—the Owner of the Church—has supreme authority over what His team does.

Every owner wants His team to look sharp, play well and win every game. Likewise, God wants the Church to win and He has a game plan. However, the team victories He has in mind for the Church are more exciting than winning a million Super Bowls.

Any self-respecting church should see itself as belonging to God. The team's highest goal, therefore, is to please the Owner. The team's greatest achievement is to bring Him abundant returns on His investment.

Unfortunately, the actions of many Christian leaders do not line up with what should be expected in a church that belongs to God. So often as leaders, both lay and clergy, we are self-possessed and determined to have a church the way we want it—or no way at all. This is a destructive attitude that needs to be corrected in light of the Cross and the Upper Room.

THE LOCAL CHURCH LEADERSHIP TEAM ORGANIZATIONAL CHART

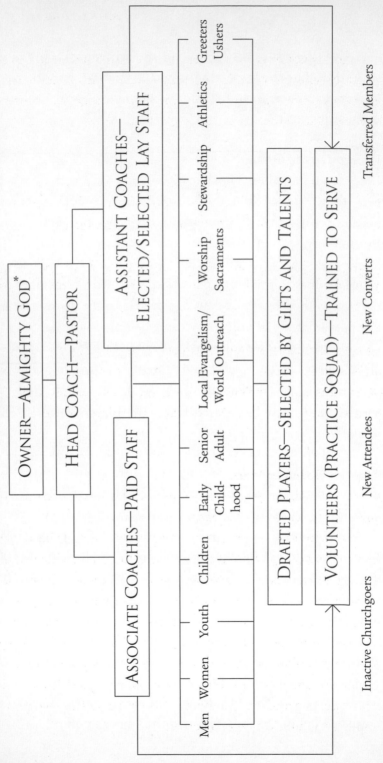

OWNER—ALMIGHTY GOD*

HEAD COACH—PASTOR

ASSISTANT COACHES—
ELECTED/SELECTED LAY STAFF

ASSOCIATE COACHES—PAID STAFF

Men Women Youth Children Early Child-hood Senior Adult Local Evangelism/ World Outreach Worship Sacraments Stewardship Athletics Greeters Ushers

DRAFTED PLAYERS—SELECTED BY GIFTS AND TALENTS

VOLUNTEERS (PRACTICE SQUAD)—TRAINED TO SERVE

Inactive Churchgoers   New Attendees   New Converts   Transferred Members

* Every member, of course, is ultimately responsible to God.

God is not only the Owner of the Church universal but also our local church. We, of course, desire favor with God; therefore, it makes sense that we would want to see our church become a favorite with Him. By becoming a favorite, we mean that our

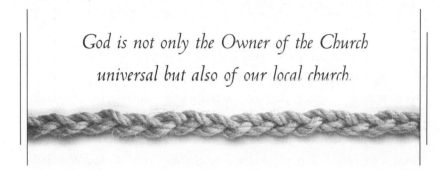

God is not only the Owner of the Church universal but also of our local church.

church is unusually loved, trusted and respected. When the team on which each player is a member becomes each player's favorite, that pleases the Owner. When it comes to God, He owns every church and must be pleased when the players on each team make the church their favorite.

Put the Coach in Place
In the NFL and other sports leagues, the owner picks a coach. In the church scenario, the coach is the pastor.

Sometimes a congregation's search for the right head coach (pastor) is a complicated process that includes reviewing resumés, calling references and interviewing the candidates. The search committee may want to observe each prospect in his previous ministry setting. Sometimes members will request a trial sermon or two. Using these procedures, a church functions like a corporation that is filling a top executive position or a university that is seeking to add a gifted professor to its faculty team. It is prudent and wise to gather accurate data and have many people provide input into the selection of a pastor.

But these steps are never enough—something more is needed. The Owner must be consulted so that He can indicate who He wants to be head coach in any particular ministry setting. His approval is significant because every pastor and every lay leader is ultimately responsible to the Owner. Seeking divine guidance for choosing leaders took place frequently in the Early Church and should be a priority now.

The guidance of the Lord may not always be easily discerned. Yet we should seek His mind and heart. Our understanding of what the Lord wants for His team comes through thoughtful reading of Scripture, passionate intercessory prayer and continual openness to providential circumstances. Divine direction may also come through informed reasoning, the wisdom of mature believers and inner impressions of lay leaders.

Always keep in mind that the head coach has a significant role in determining a team's effectiveness. For this reason, choosing the right leader may be the most important decision that the members of a church ever make. We must deliberate thoughtfully and obediently and with utter openness to God's direction. Selecting a pastor is not about what we want; rather, it is about what God wants.

Picking the right head coach is important, because he stands at the center of a congregation's influence and ministry. Similar to a football coach, the pastor recruits players, develops the team, trains its members and calls most of the plays. He knows his players personally; therefore, he knows when to shift a halfback to a fullback or when to send in a substitute. The winning coach does his work through others whom he has trained and conditioned so that they can give their best effort. Likewise, the pastor is to equip the saints (see Eph. 4:12).

Allow the Coach to Work

After the head coach is firmly in place, he has three significant functions:

1. to set the mission or game plan,
2. to choose a team to help reach the Owner's expectations, and
3. to serve as a servant/shepherd and a teacher/preacher.

In all three functions, the head coach must keep his eye on the goal—to be pleasing in the sight of the Owner, God Himself. The head coach must understand these functions and perform them well. Lay leaders must do all they can to enable pastors to accomplish these three functions.

Once the Owner has had a significant say in selecting a head coach, the coaching staff is then assembled. Choosing, recruiting, securing, developing, inspiring and discipling team players stands as the most important of all the coach's tasks, because everything else depends on the makeup and abilities of the team. In the NFL, there is an assistant coach for nearly every position—kickers, receivers, linemen, offensive units and defensive units each have their own coaches—every position has a coach. In the church it may be difficult to follow this model—but maybe not.

Follow our reasoning: In the multiple-staff congregation, the head coach will need to determine the priorities. Will they be youth, music, missions, outreach, senior adults—what? The areas that have the highest priorities will get paid staff; those with lesser significance or that have well-gifted church members available will be given to laymen who will serve as assistant coaches.

You may be thinking, *That is nice for megachurches, but my church has only one pastor and we cannot afford a paid staff.* Now we are on the right track.

The average church is composed of about 90 adults. In the United States, on any Sunday, 35 percent of the congregations have no more than one paid professional staff member. This is where the laymen come in. If the lay leadership of the church communities will step in and assume the role of assistant coaches, the local body will flourish.

Accomplish Ministry—In a New Way

Let's propose a way to exponentially multiply the achievement of every church.

What if everyone chosen to serve on the governing body of a local congregation had a specific ministry responsibility and commitment to serve on that board? For example, a 10-person leadership team might assign a member of their group to coach ministries for each of the following: (1) men, (2) women, (3) teens, (4) children, (5) senior adults, (6) world outreach, (7) local evangelism, (8) worship and sacraments, (9) athletics and (10) finance and building. Other areas could be added or subtracted, as the coaching team sees fit.

When a church uses this model, each team member has a specific ministry responsibility. An obligation and a privilege nudges, or forces, her to move from the detached bleacher mindset to the white-heat, sweaty intensity of winning the game. When each person has a role, it is difficult for any team player to criticize the game plan, because she helped design it. Moreover, taking ministry seriously becomes contagious as team members watch each other take on the challenges of their particular responsibility.

If a particular church is large enough to have a full-time staff in addition to the senior pastor, then the dynamics change. The other paid staff will be designated as assistant coaches—not coaches—and their roles will be more specifically defined. They will become area pastors, in addition to their other responsibilities. The city, or congregation, pie will be divided 2, 3 or even 10 ways, depending upon its size and the number on the staff. In this model, every paid staff member is responsible for the oversight of a geographic section. Then the other coaches (unpaid laymen whom we will call lay coaches) are aligned to a paid staff—but are still responsible for their specific assignments. For example, if there is a full-time music leader (assistant coach), then the lay coach assigned to work with music ministry will be responsible to help in recruiting or will take on other duties that the assistant coach deems appropriate.

Draft a Team of Players

Once a coaching staff is in place, what comes next? The draft! Anyone who has coached in a youth league is familiar with drafting procedures. In the church setting, we can draw a parallel: After the head coach has been determined, the assistant coaches (paid staff) hired and the lay coaches (lay leaders) selected, then the franchise (church) is ready to start its draft.

The players to be designated to particular areas of need and service are the church members. Every congregation is divided into families, and each family member in good standing is given a number. Those in the congregation who are not members or who are not officially connected with the church are put on an alternate list to be considered after the first rounds of drafting are completed. The drafting, or assigning as we sometimes call it in the Church, process is necessary to ensure that some people in the church do not wear themselves out with more jobs than one person should handle. The coaching staff should determine the policy regarding how much responsibility can be given to any one member. This plan solves most personnel problems, particularly the common dilemma of not having anyone to lead or work in one or two of the less-desirable but much-needed aspects of ministry.

As the coaches work through the list of available people, they should consider each person's gifting. Gifting can be defined as the talents and abilities God has given each individual for service. What a sense of strength comes to us when we know God created us with special abilities He wants us to use in His kingdom. And what a relief to know we do not have to be exactly like anyone else.

The apostle Paul delightfully described the gifting of every believer:

> Each of us finds our meaning and function as a part of his body. But as a chopped-off finger or cut-off toe we wouldn't amount to much, would we? So since we find ourselves fashioned into all these excellently formed and marvelously functioning parts in Christ's body, let's just go ahead and be what we were made to be, without enviously or pridefully comparing ourselves with each other, or trying to be something we aren't (Rom. 12:4-5, *THE MESSAGE*).

A process for discovering and deploying spiritual gifts must be developed so that every parishioner knows what God has prepared him or her to do. Moreover, it will be helpful for coaches to be aware of an individual's gifts before drafting him or her to serve in a specific assignment. The gifts are explained in five New Testament passages: Romans 12:6-8; 1 Corinthians 12:7-10; 1 Corinthians 12:28-30; Ephesians 4:11; and 1 Peter 4:9-11. The following summary lists the basic gifts:

1. Preach
2. Serve
3. Encourage
4. Teach
5. Give
6. Show mercy
7. Lead and administer
8. Evangelize
9. Show hospitality
10. Have faith
11. Heal
12. Pray
13. Be cross-cultural
14. Exhibit discernment
15. Help
16. Exhort
17. Pastor
18. Show mercy
19. Be wise
20. Be an apostle

Each member of the coaching team looks over the list and prays for the draft session.

Who drafts first? In most sports leagues—the NFL, the WNBA or the local little league—the weakest team from the previous year drafts first. The keys to the selection process are unselfishness and an assistant coach's commitment to the strengthening and continued development of the whole church. Leaders must first ask these questions: Where are the needs? Who could best fill the needed openings? Where can the gifts of the membership be most effectively placed for the greatest achievement of the gospel?

The apostle Paul advises, "Those parts of the body that seem to be weaker are indispensable, and the parts that we think are less honorable we treat with special honor" (1 Cor. 12:22-23). Therefore, we first match the greatest need with the most capable human resources God gives us and then adequately attend to all other areas of ministry.

Here is how the drafting process works: A large piece of paper or white board is placed on the wall in the meeting area. Every ministry-related position is posted. When the draft begins, the head coach highlights the job openings and calls upon the assistant coaches under whose area the positions fall to nominate church attendees to fill the positions. Sometimes assistant coaches trade draft choices just as teams do in professional sports leagues. Their main objective is to get the best person possible to fill each ministry slot.

What if you already have someone in a slot, but the duties of the position do not allow the person to use her best gifting? Negotiate! Talk about it! Sometimes you will need permission from the one already serving to even consider a change. That is where loyalty among the coaches is crucial. They must be fully committed to the Owner of the Church, loyal to the mission of the church, faithful to the vision of the head coach and dutiful to the unity of the body. Scripture gives us the goal: "All the believers were together and had everything in common" (Acts 2:44).

The drafting continues until every member of the coach's staff and each member of the congregation has an assignment. Do not forget: Greeters in the parking lot can be just as important as Sunday School leaders. The early childhood caregiver is just as vital as a member of the worship team. It is up to the coaching staff to sell the team members on their individual and corporate value.

Barna helps us understand this point:

> The church's culture must change, people must understand and own the change, key leaders have to model the practice, and the implementation has to be carefully constructed to facilitate effectiveness—the church must have the patience to allow the plan to work. . . . It may take two or three years to complete the transition from solo-based leadership to team-based lay-driven leadership.[3]

In reality, today no more than 20 percent of any congregation volunteers for Christian service, even to serve in the most prestigious positions. Think how much more could be done if we raised that percentage a few points. What a difference it would make! That is one of the glories of the coach-team paradigm—it provides the opportunity and option for those who might not otherwise volunteer to at least consider the possibility. It creates an environment where there are of lot of people who are very committed to Christian service. It puts assistant coaches in a strong position to help recruit workers. And it makes everyone believe something good is happening because of the increased participation.

THE CHALLENGES

1. Sell the Concept

The team model and pattern of leadership and service will bring about drastic changes for many churches, but those changes are improvements that make a local congregation more effective and closer to the original model of service to Christ found in the Early Church. Therefore, the concept must be carefully considered, prayed about and promoted. For some people this model will appear to be a violation of their trust; for others it will mean increased personal involvement. Take at least six months to launch the program. Choose and start training your coaches before you even think about the draft aspect of this model.

2. Train the Team

The head coach must invest his time in the assistant coaches and the lay coaches, always being careful to seek the will of the Owner. He must assure them that he will stand with them all the way to the Super Bowl. That means he must create and execute a well-planned mission and clearly communicate his vision. He must establish well-defined roles and give the best possible human effort, and then he must surrender the total program to the power of God. A head coach who will not commit to total involvement with his coaching staff will soon become the outsider.

3. Create Unity and Loyalty

From the beginning of the process, everyone must understand that the head coach will be the leader. Mutiny is not an option and selfishness cannot be tolerated, because division will destroy the program. When disagreements arise, they must be dealt with in the spirit of Christ and in the best interests of the church family. Differences must be discussed and dealt with quickly. The moment dissension and conflict are allowed to fester, the leadership team model unravels. Anyone who cannot be loyal to the head coach should step aside and allow others to serve. More than anything else, shared vision and unity permeated the Early Church.

4. Pray Together

Just as any courageous enterprise is impossible without the power of prayer, so it is with a creative, innovative leadership team model. The new program should be unveiled in a prayerful setting—maybe at a retreat and among just a few trusted people. All further meetings must also be laid before the Lord. We must trust His Word: "'Not by might nor by power, but by my Spirit,' says the LORD Almighty" (Zech. 4:6). So many well-intentioned dreams and ideas in the local church are paralyzed because those involved are not willing to pay the price of prolonged prayer. It is hard work. Sometimes people do not pray because they do not want what God wants.

5. Expect Criticism

Remember all the opposition Nehemiah received when he was on the wall? From both inside and out, he battled the naysayers until one day they just had to say, "Let us start rebuilding" (Neh. 2:18). Immediately his coworkers began to build, but the critics mocked

If we are going to have an impact for the gospel, we must reverse course and make it to the Super Bowl.

and ridiculed them. Nehemiah answered, "The God of heaven will give us success. We his servants will start rebuilding" (Neh. 2:20).

Church work is risky. The commitment to the local body is still very tepid. Forty percent of the adult population attend church; 38 percent read the Bible; only 20 percent donate money. Fewer than 4 out of 10 share their faith.[4] We live in troubled times. If we are going to have an impact for the gospel, we must reverse course and make it to the Super Bowl.

People and the devil will fill you with thoughts of self-doubt. You will feel alone as head coach. They will ask, "Why don't you just let things stay the way they are?" But you cannot! The stakes are too high. The battle is the Lord's. You must join Him.

6. Anticipate Attrition

Along the way, some people will quit the team. Whenever you determine to move beyond the ordinary, you will come face-to-face with those who are enthusiastic at first and then, like Demas in the Bible, desert you (see 2 Tim. 4:10). That is the human predicament, but do not despair. God always provides the manpower necessary to get the job done.

On an NFL team there are two separate groups in addition to the regulars. They are called practice, or taxi, squads. Individuals on these units are committed to the team and share the vision of the head coach but are still on the fringe of the fellowship or not ready to make a sold-out promise to the leadership team—but they have huge potential.

Every team needs a practice squad. This is where you place people in training. Often these people are new converts who want to mature. Sometimes they are young people who have faced difficulties and made huge mistakes in their lives but have now found renewal and deliverance in Christ. They may need some time to put all the pieces together, but they bring excitement to the team. They are wide-eyed with hope. Bring them along, because they will need someone to walk beside them, pick them up when they fall, talk to them when they are lonely and reassure them when they are tempted to return to their former way of life.

Use your worship services to let these people tell of their new lives. Expose them to the love of the congregation. Help them realize their potential. Then when some in leadership decide they have had enough, that they no longer want to be on the team, you will have players from the practice squad to bring up.

THE GAME BEGINS

Having played a little football, I (H. B.) can still remember game day: The fellowship and camaraderie that existed in the locker room prior to taking the field motivated the team, those last-minute pep talks by the coach, the assistant coaches making their way from player to player with a reminder or insight and the sound of cleats on the runway before the coach led us onto the field inspired us to play the best game we could. The people in the stands cheered, the band played, the pep squad rallied the supporters and before we knew it, the ball was in the air and the game was under way. What a thrill! Coaches, assistant coaches and the players were all on the same page—we all had one goal in mind: a championship!

We can seek to join the unity of vision in our churches *for the cause of Christ*. We can work to see God's plan come to fruition as the Holy Spirit leads and empowers us.

Hopefully what we have written in this book will encourage you to reach beyond what you can easily grasp. We want you to recruit the best people you can to join you and be a leader of peace and model unity among your people. Pray constantly and challenge others to join you. Dream dreams you have never dared to dream—and have a positive attitude! You have embarked on a mission that only those of great faith will ever realize. You will be on the winning team.

Go for it!

RENEWAL STRATEGIES FOR LAY LEADERS: A NEW PARADIGM

This proposed new strategy for fulfilling partnerships with lay leaders will help God and the local congregation fulfill these three important phases of ministry: the local congregation will prosper, the need for recruitment by pastors for new workers will be significantly lower, and the fellowship that grows out of serving together will be rich for many years to come. Let's review, implement and rejoice over what God is doing.

1. Organize your church's governing board into a team of leaders.
2. Do your part to move every decision maker into the field of action.
3. Question whether a church can be faithful without achievement.
4. Recognize God as the Owner of your church and your leadership team.
5. Commit to the principle that the Owner always has the right to have the last word.
6. Remind the team that the Owner has a lot to say about choosing the coach.
7. Use the draft to make sure that no one is overworked and everyone has an assignment.
8. Implement the Jesus team model, even though it represents a drastic change for many churches.
9. Use criticism for self-evaluation.
10. Dream dreams you never dared to dream before now.

Notes
1. Barna Research Group, news release, Ventura, CA, June 26, 2000.
2. Ibid.
3. Ibid.
4. Ibid.

A common mistake is to believe that because individuals are all on the same team, they all think alike and act alike. Not so. The purpose of a team is to make the strengths of each person effective, and his or her weaknesses irrelevant.

PETER F. DRUCKER, *MANAGING THE NON-PROFIT ORGANIZATION*

CHAPTER 2

SHARPEN YOUR SKILLS

WHAT IT TAKES TO BELONG TO A WORLD-CLASS TEAM

Builder and Sustainer of the Church,
Empower us for the work You have for us.
Open our wills to understand Your purposes for
us.
Show us how to more fully love our fellow team
members.
Put the eternal in our steps and the applause of
heaven in our hearts.
Amen.

Professional athletics is big business and seems to be getting bigger all the time. Stadiums dwarf cathedrals. Star players' salaries shock our sensibilities. Gossip, statistics and standings fill sports sections of newspapers every day. Freeway traffic thins to a trickle when Super Bowl games are in progress because fans are glued to their TV sets. There are cable networks that air nothing but sports: nonstop football, basketball, baseball, hockey, tennis, soccer, kayaking, skateboarding and all sorts of extreme events that did not even exist a few years ago. Kids beg for shirts and jackets that bear the names and numbers of their favorite players. Armchair critics yell at television screens when coaches make difficult decisions and fans rag players from the stands. Sports saturate our society.

While few of us have had experience playing on high-caliber sports teams, most of us have had team-playing experience. Some of us have been volunteer firefighters, participated in church or high school athletics or joined parent-teacher organizations. We have sung in choirs, enrolled in support groups and competed in Little League games. We must show teamwork at work, at school, in the marketplace and even at home. Many of us are so involved in youth sports that we completely understand what the working mother means when she says, "I am a soccer transportation specialist." For her, just getting to the game requires teamwork.

When we look at team participation that way, it seems that nearly everyone has had some experience. For some people, being part of a team was an exhilarating high; for others it was a disappointing flop. Whatever experience members of our churches have had with teamwork, we need to use them when we form our teams.

Define "Team"

A definition of "team" might be helpful before we go any further. For the purpose of this book, a team is any group of persons who work together to achieve common goals that make use of the members' individual giftedness.

To sort through what it means to be part of the decision-making team at church, we can go back to our other team experiences and assess our past involvement and then determine what insights and skills can cross over into the work of the church. We should ponder some questions: *What makes being a member of the church team unique? How can we keep difficulties we have encountered in other groups from undermining the church team? What did we do well in other groups that we can also do well as a team member at church?*

Let's start at the starting line.

Our journey toward becoming a church team member begins by assessing the kind of people we are—our commitments, values and attitudes. We should ask ourselves if character-shaping issues like forgiveness, hope and trust are current in our lives. We

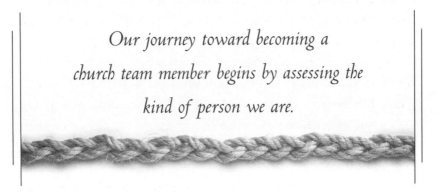

Our journey toward becoming a church team member begins by assessing the kind of person we are.

should measure the current level of our spiritual development and motivation. And we should ask ourselves probing questions about how things are going in our family lives.

To help evaluate our growth and self-understanding, why not develop a personal team member credo? This would clearly state what we really believe. The following statements might serve as a springboard for developing such a statement:

1. I believe in the gospel of Jesus Christ.
2. I believe God owns the Church.
3. I believe pastors are God's gift to His Church and have been given spiritual authority over His Church.
4. I believe being a Christian is the best possible way to live.
5. I believe that the Church is both human and divine.
6. I believe in involvement in Christian service.

7. I believe in asking questions and asking for help.

8. I believe most problems can be solved with shared ideas and teamwork.

9. I believe in speaking my mind and allowing the same privilege to others.

10. I believe the Bible is the infallible Word of God.

11. I believe in admitting mistakes and accepting blame.

12. I believe in doing my share of the work to implement decisions.

13. I believe in supporting the Body of Christ with my financial giving and my physical energy.

14. I believe leadership requires more than charisma.

15. I believe in the potential of people, including myself and my pastor.

16. I believe everyone wants to find ways to make his life count.[1]

Question Assumptions

You should debate with yourself when questions about church-team leadership arise because some assumptions you hold are exactly right, but some of them are very wrong, or shaky at best. Several commonly accepted assumptions need to be studied thoroughly and rejected.

Assumption: Election or appointment makes a person a leader.
Reality: Being elected to serve is only the open door to becoming a leader.

Assumption: Power and authority are to be hoarded.
Reality: A person cannot be an authentic leader until after he becomes a true servant. Jesus explained,

"Whoever wants to become great among you must be your servant" (Matt. 20:26).

Assumption: Lay leaders must control the pastor.

Reality: Dialogue, collegial interaction, shared ideas, thoughtful negotiations, heated debate, committee reports and board action are all needed and useful. But no church prospers spiritually that does not allow its pastor to lead.

Assumption: Status quo must be defended.

Reality: The nature of the work of God is progressive, at the cutting edge and achievement oriented. Do not miss the exhilaration and adventure at the front lines.

Assumption: Talk is action.

Reality: If everything recorded in the minutes of church decision-making groups was suddenly implemented tomorrow, the world would not know what to do. The old proverb is right: After all is said and done, not enough is done. Voting on an issue is not ministry. Action has to follow in order to produce achievement.

GET PAST DESTRUCTIVE NOTIONS

At this critical moment in human history when the Church is needed more than ever, the work of God in thousands of places moves at a snail's pace or has ground to an embarrassing halt. Our leaders have nothing to say that matters and give themselves to causes that are too puny for what Scripture says about the Church. The underlying causes for this sad condition can often be traced to leaders who hold mistaken views about their task or leaders who fail to lead.

Election or appointment to an important assignment does strange things to some people, and they seem to suffer personality changes—seldom for the better. The changes show in statements such as "I'm in control" or "I can't have friends who are not on my level."

Tradition Defenders

Some lay leaders think that they have the responsibility to defend traditional methodologies. On this subject, humorist Will Rogers was right: "The past has never been half what it used to be and never has been." Hands clutching the status quo can never be opened to receive new opportunities.

Trivia Protectors

Sometimes leaders start irrational battles over trivia. How silly to have wars in church, a place God intended for peacemakers to meet. Keep peace and work for unity. Every church fuss sabotages someone's faith and subverts a congregation's influence on its members and in its community.

Law Enforcers

Sometimes leaders become in-residence police officers who make sure the rules are kept—rules such as who gets to use the church facilities, who has a master key and what time the pastor comes to the office each day. These type of people usually behave like patrolmen who enjoy writing tickets. Innovation drives them crazy. Policing the church in this way often leads to legalism and diverts the focus away from faith, love and transformation.

People who believe they must be protectors are another version of the church cop. These types of people generally feel that they must guard something, though they usually are not sure what. They try to guard money, doctrine and tradition without realizing that protection does not come from more rules; instead, it comes from more Christlikeness. Sometimes protectors are so vocal that other team members let them have their way so that no one has to listen to any more of their pious drivel.

Positive-Negative Thinkers

Some lay leaders develop positive-negative personalities. While trying to think like Stephen Covey, Robert Schuller and Norman Vincent Peale all rolled into one personality, they are positive about everything but with a negative twist. A typical response might be, "I am enthused that our new building will help us serve hundreds of new people, providing the bank doesn't foreclose."

Veto Specialists

Leaders who have a penchant for the veto are also a problem. They see their task as showing up to vote an issue down, often without being able to explain why. This mistaken view usually turns lay leaders into irritable benchwarmers, because nobody wants to follow them.

Passive-Aggressive Troublemakers

The passive-aggressive attitude assumed by some lay leaders invariably causes problems among the ranks. This type of person accepts other team members with a feigned friendship but ruins reputation outside the meetings. They undermine morale by their actions—then they wonder why no teamwork exists.

Special-Interest Representatives

A few leaders see themselves as representatives of special-interest groups, perhaps the youth, senior citizens or women. They feel obligated to speak for a minority group, a lot like the United States senator who tacks a farm subsidy amendment on to a national homeland security bill. While the interests of all groups within the church need to be represented, heard and addressed, team players cannot let the priorities of one group negatively affect the overall vision and goals of the church. It would be counterproductive to have a congregation that fit all of the needs of single fathers but never reached out to seniors or high schoolers.

DEVELOP WHOLESOME PERSPECTIVES

Decision-making group members can maximize their effectiveness by checking their concepts of lay leadership against the following wholesome perspectives of highly effective church lay leaders:

1. Be an Authentic Christian

Work at becoming a great Christian. The godly life in Christ Jesus, much more than a duty or pleasing possibility, is an amazing adventure. An intentional closeness with Jesus is its main ingredient. More than a lofty, ungraspable theory, this relation-

The godly life in Christ Jesus, much more than a duty or pleasing possibility, is an amazing adventure.

ship provides blazing new insights as it questions old notions. It provides stalwart strengths and helps us use our difficulties and disappointments. Like an old mystic once said, "God lights the way of the Christian with joy, love, peace and faith."

The significance of this personal faith is summarized in an observation about football teams made by legendary Green Bay Packers' coach Vince Lombardi:

> When we place our dependence in God, we are unencumbered and we have no worry. In fact, we may even be reckless, insofar as our part in the production is concerned. This confidence, this sureness of action, is both contagious and an aid to the perfect action. The rest is in the hands of God, and this is the same God, gentlemen, who has won all His battles up to now.[2]

Leonardo da Vinci shines a powerful light on this service issue:

> Iron rusts from disuse, stagnant water loses its purity, and in cold weather becomes frozen; even so does inaction sap the vigors of the mind. It is also true about faith that fools itself into inaction.[3]

A lasting, living definition of greatness was established on Maundy Thursday when Jesus washed the disciples' feet. That day He demonstrated that serving stands at the top of the Father's list of priorities. Since then, it is the assigned privilege of authentic leaders to actually serve the people that they lead. If we want to be this kind of a leader, then when we see a need, we need to grab a towel and get to work.

In our personal pilgrimage of faith, we must resist the temptation to become professional Christians, those who become so involved in the institutional side of the church that they never get their hands dirty or their muscles sore. Professional Christians serve on committees and boards but never involve themselves in the actual flesh-and-blood, do-or-die ministry. They are like members of hospital boards who never push a gurney or hold the hand of a dying patient.

We must live holy lives. True spirituality is living out the beauty of Jesus—the One the Church represents—in every dimension of life. Among the most needed traits for a church leader is to be able to sing and mean, "It is well with my soul." When we reach this point in our pilgrimage, there is no room for doublespeak, preening piety, self-seeking pride or an arrogant show of authority—just authenticity, integrity, grace and inner beauty.

Great Christians who enjoy such an adventurous walk with God are needed as lay leaders. Do not settle for just being a member of a corporate board when you could be a grace-filled representative of the living Christ on the decision-making group at your church.

2. Emphasize Mission Focus

Do everything you can to keep your church leadership team focused on Christ's mission in the world. Such a focus provides a delivery system and a sword—a delivery system to carry the load and a sword to cut away trivia. Theologian Emil Brunner put it well: "The church exists by mission as fire exists by burning."[4]

Mission, properly understood, ignites imagination, creativity and energy. That is why every decision-making group needs someone who can communicate the congregation's mission accurately, competently and frequently.

Every church decision-making group works better when it knows what the church is supposed to be and do. Burt Nanus, in his book *Visionary Leaders,* has a powerful insight from business practices that church leaders can use: "Leaders live the vision by making all their actions and behaviors consistent with it and by creating a sense of urgency and passion for its attainment."[5]

3. Value Process as Part of Achievement

Leading is almost never a single event; rather, it is a process. Effective leaders learn to respect the process that leads to achievement because it often develops and unites people. Leading does not accomplish its purpose in a day. Neither can it get to the right destination if it goes in the wrong direction. However, it is wise to remember that doing what the Church has always done will likely produce the same results it has always produced. For most churches, this means falling short of its full potential.

President John F. Kennedy's observation can apply to the church: "We are inclined to think that if we watch a football game or a baseball game, we have taken part in it."[6] Merely attending a board meeting does not mean you are helping to build the kingdom of Christ.

Attending a meeting, discussing a task, making a motion and voting are all part of serving in a decision-making group. But someone has to follow through and do the work after decisions are made.

Insist upon achievement. Thousands of lay leaders have excused themselves and their churches by saying, "We are not responsible for results but for being faithful." If a church has no achievement, perhaps its leaders should reexamine their ministry to be sure they are doing the right things.

4. Call the Bluff

Every church has obstacles that mesmerize its leaders, sometimes for many years. Some hindrances actually become glass ceilings on progress. The excuses run the gamut: Somebody is against it. Our location hampers us. Our reputation is bad. Our pastor is too old. Our pastor is too young. Our parking lot is too inconvenient. It will cost too much! Make your own list and then challenge each item on it. Every church that progresses has someone who challenges and tears down barriers.

Take courage from evangelist Vance Havner: "There is a reckless, almost fierce, faith that laughs in the teeth of circumstances and shouts, like Paul in the storm, 'I believe God,' and affirms, though a legion of demons mock, 'Let God be true but every man a liar.' "[7]

Cultivate an atmosphere of faith. Come to every meeting with a desire to nourish the inner life of every team member. Make it a personal rule that before every committee or board meeting you pray for guidance, wisdom and the ability to demonstrate the spirit of Christ to those with whom you serve.

5. Maximize the Meaning of Service

Service is a gift to be opened, enjoyed and given away. Share service satisfactions. Jesus is an example of what we mean. He multiplied His ministry by commissioning and sending out the disciples to do the same works He was doing. Meanwhile, He continued His earthly ministry, showing us an ideal blend of working through others while continuing to work Himself.

Service done in the name of Jesus is a friend to be welcomed, never resisted or ignored. T. S. Eliot enjoyed saying, "We have had the experience but missed the meaning."[8] That is how many people tend to serve in the church—do not fall into this trap. It will shrivel your soul and bore those whom you touch.

6. Cherish People

People are the church's main business and greatest asset. Yet too many churches have no people. One Sunday, I (Neil) attended the state cathedral in Stockholm, Sweden—only 64 people were present at the main worship service. How sad. It is easy to develop an institutional maintenance mentality that forgets the church exists for people.

When we multiply love, we begin to reach the hearts of those around us. Love for God, our neighbors and ourselves stands at the center of the church's message. Love is God's specialty. He is love. Therefore, effective ministry flows out of love. The way love moves from the heart of God through us was beautifully explained by Mother Teresa:

> We must be loved by God first, and only then can we give love to others. For us to want to give love to others, we must be full of God's love to give. God acts this way. It is He who moves us all to do what we are doing, and if we feel His love for us, then this love emanates from us.[9]

Love cannot be legislated or mandated, but it increases in gigantic proportions in any church when one or two leaders decide to be more loving and lovable. When this happens, love rapidly spreads throughout the whole fellowship.

7. Understand Change and Commit to Progress

Often resistance to change is a cover for a loss of nerve or lack of faith. To counter this tendency, we must learn to welcome innovation. Christ was an innovator who often did the unexpected. He did not keep the Sabbath in ways in which religious leaders expected Him to keep it. He taught His followers to love their enemies and befriend sinners. He told hearers that they must be slaves if they were to be free and that they needed to die in order to live. To achieve without taking risks is as impossible as to live without being born.

Although change is neither a friend nor a foe, it is always with us, like taxes and the threat of death. In fact, as we move further into the twenty-first century, the pace of change keeps increasing. The Botswani proverb is right: "Today always comes before tomorrow."[10]

Decisions made today or left unmade today will determine the future of a church. Football coach Don Shula's wise advice applies to life and to the church: "There is no point in sticking with a game plan that's not working."[11]

8. Listen to Others

Truth is often communicated as much by body language as by actual words. When conversing with someone, concentrate on what the other person says and what she means. Too often people use the time when they are supposed to be listening to build a defense or to formulate a reply. One experienced pastor estimated that members of his church decision-making group listened less than 75 percent of the time. No wonder that congregation had many misunderstandings among its members.

Restudy your stand on an issue when you meet resistance. Perhaps your opinion has weak spots you have overlooked. It might help to make a simple request, such as: "The issue looks this way to me, but since you do not agree, please help me see your point of view. I want to understand your position." Most often the other person will explain her view, and both people will benefit from the conversation.

9. Pursue Things That Last

An effective leader gives up the passing and preserves the timeless—and knows the difference. It is not of value to participate in lengthy debates, resist new methods or endlessly fiddle with a small part of a new idea. Forcing innovators to swim upstream in molasses is never productive and ultimately leads to a weak or dying organization.

Know the difference between method and mission. Methods and strategies must always change to fit new days and new ways, but a church's mission is permanent and should be used as the foundation for determining methodologies. More churches divide over methods than over doctrine or Scripture.

A person who stretches himself to consider a new way of thinking and doing will likely never fully return to the original way. The poet Ralph Waldo Emerson teaches us a lot about teamwork:

Men grind and grind in the mill of a truism, and nothing comes out but what is put in. But the moment they desert the tradition for a spontaneous thought, then poetry, wit, hope, virtue, learning, anecdote, all flock to their aid.[12]

10. Value and Build Trust

Trust embodies honesty, fairness and respect for followers. In his thoughtful book *Jesus on Leadership*, Gene Wilkes explains how important trust is to a congregation's leadership team: "Trust between church leaders and members allows the work of mission to be done. Trust tends to destroy an atmosphere of control and creates an air of freedom. Trust allows a leader to lead."[13] A true leader is always trustworthy.

NOW, GO TO WORK

For lay leaders it is time to achieve the mission of your leadership teams. Think of the elements for achievement that are already present in your church. You have the redeeming gospel with its

The challenge is to find ways to take the gospel into every aspect of daily life.

transforming power. Spiritually needy people are all around you. When you activate your team and move forward with God's plan, you can bring that gospel to those needy people.

Do not sleep through the revolution going on all around you. You play a bad joke on yourself if you try to believe these are not profoundly revolutionary days. The challenge is to find ways to take the gospel into every aspect of daily life. And that task will either be done by local churches or not at all. Let's rub the sleep out of our eyes and make your church revolutionary.

CHALLENGE THE DREAMERS

God wants to build a winning and joyful team in your church that uses all the skills that its members bring from every team experience they have ever had.

But God has something bigger, nobler and eternal for this team to accomplish. God wants your church team to dream dreams and see visions. He wants your church to think globally and act locally—to realize that the world cannot be won without strong local congregations making it happen. This team realizes that N. Gordon Cosby is correct with his discouraging words: "The church in many of its expressions seems fat and bloated and mired down in almost complete paralysis."[14]

The church does not need to remain ineffective and wither away in this fashion. If it has teams that have members who see new possibilities of what can be done for the King, the mission can be achieved. To accomplish this the church must have leaders who will voluntarily step up to the challenge, report for duty and declare: "Here I am. Send me. I'll go. I'll assume the responsibility."

Let your work on God's team be inspired by the old story Rufus Jones told about a little boy playing on the deck of a ship plowing through a pitching storm at sea. When a passenger asked the boy if he was afraid, he replied, "I'm not afraid because my father is captain of this ship."

Your Father is the Captain, and all is well.

Notes

1. Alan Cox, *Straight Talk for Monday Mornings* (New York: Wiley, 1990), pp. 315-316.
2. Vince Lombardi, Jr., *What It Takes to Win* (New York: McGraw Hill, 2001), p. 57.
3. Leonardo da Vinci, quoted in Ted Goodman, *Forbes Book of Business Quotations* (New York: Black Dog and Leventhal Publishers, 1997), p. 29.
4. Hannah Ward and Jennifer Wild, comp., *Doubleday Christian Quotation Collection* (New York: Doubleday, 1998), p. 244.
5. Burt Nanus, quoted in Gene Wilkes, *Jesus on Leadership* (Wheaton, IL: Tyndale, 1998), p. 154.
6. John F. Kennedy, quoted in Goodman, *Forbes Book of Business Quotations*, p. 789.
7. Vance Havner, *Day by Day* (Grand Rapids, MI: Baker, 1953), p. 147.
8. T. S. Eliot, *The Oxford Dictionary of Phrase, Saying and Quotation*, ed. Elizabeth Knowles (London: Oxford University Press, 1997), p. 160.
9. Mother Teresa, *A Simple Faith* (New York: Ballatine Books, 1996), p. 80.
10. Venice Johnson, ed., *Heart Full of Grace* (New York: Simon and Schuster, 1997), p. 202.
11. Ken Blanchard and Don Shula, *Little Book of Coaching* (New York: Harper Collins Publishers, Inc., 2001), p. 59.
12. Ralph Waldo Emerson, quoted in Cox, *Straight Talk for Monday Mornings*, p. 97.
13. Wilkes, *Jesus on Leadership*, p. 71.
14. N. Gordon Cosby, *By Grace Transformed* (New York: Crossroad Publishing, 1999), p. 15.

*God pursues the leader relentlessly; searching for
entrance into every area of the leader's heart,
ambitions, emotions, passions, fears, loves, prejudices,
assumptions, character and behaviors.*

REGGIE MCNEAL, *A WORK OF HEART*

CHAPTER 3

SERVICE, SUBMISSION AND SACRIFICE

HOW TO REPLICATE JESUS' TEAM-BUILDING SPIRIT

Lord of the Church,
  So that our team may replicate Your way of
    serving,
  break our hearts with the needs around us,
  grant us joy in serving with others,
  teach us to value gifts others bring to our team
  and honor us with a healthy church.
  Amen.

Jesus amazed the world with His leadership skills. No one before Him had used service, submission and sacrifice to attract and develop a world-class team. But He did. Furthermore, He surprised everyone when He used grace and love to sculpt the disciples into a winning team. As He developed His team, He showed why He is the greatest leader of all time.

The leadership strategies Jesus used—service, submission, sacrifice, grace and love—surprised the Romans who ruled the world with military might. He also amazed the Greeks who valued culture as the cornerstone of civilization. And He surprised the Jews who lived by strict observance of the laws and could not believe that *their* Messiah would die on a cross.

People in every generation have been and continue to be amazed when they discover that the servant Savior came to Earth and put on flesh and bones so that He could save sinners and serve the people of all nations. What a contrast Christianity offers when compared to other religions that have deities who are said to be far away and disinterested!

THE TEAM OWNER WITH A SELF-GIVING ATTITUDE

Jesus' way of leading is so different from what we find around us today. Fueled by an unquenchable desire for power, clever leaders too often posture, intimidate and scheme their way into control. Their success, however, comes at a big cost.

Power addiction is a dreadful disease of the soul that always takes its toll.

Even one team member infested by this contagious virus can cripple most efforts of a whole church. The selfish ambition to control the church fools power seekers. They believe the subtle lie that being in charge and having their own way will bring satisfaction, but it never does for very long. More often than not, those who pull strings to get control find that after they get their wish, a gnawing sense of inner doubt follows them around like a mangy hound. Like every other kind of thief, they suffer when their memory keeps reminding them of how they got where they are.

How they gained their power begins to bother them. Next, they find it increasingly difficult to pray. Then clouds of self-doubt and suspicion hover over all of their relationships. They feel alone and insecure. Often the situation becomes more desperate when it is discovered that they are poorly prepared for the task they so eagerly sought.

Meanwhile, the position they schemed to get suffers severe damage. The work flounders as the leader tries to maintain control. Sadly, the unspoken history of many churches, colleges and parachurch organizations shows they have been severely crippled by this type of power addict. In the end this pathetic maneuvering can be compared to a rich man with no athletic ability trying to buy himself a place on the roster of an NFL team.

By contrast, Jesus invested self-giving love in a team of people whose influence continues to this day, 2,000 years later. He did not write a book or incorporate His ministry with the government. He did not travel the globe or network with friends. He did not buy a business or water down His message. Instead, He spent 90 percent of His time developing a team He hoped would lead the way He did. And what they accomplished is history.

Jesus' self-giving leadership still attracts people; its warmth draws them like a magnet.

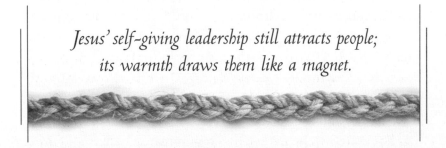

Jesus' self-giving leadership still attracts people; its warmth draws them like a magnet. By His way of leading He demonstrates that the basis of world-impacting influence is selfless service. He shows that selfless service liberates while control wounds the human spirit. Self-serving leaders, on the contrary, cause churches to plateau or even decline. On the other hand, whenever Jesus' model of leadership is put into action, it makes the

church unique among organizations, and growth generally follows.

HOW THE FIRST SERVANT TEAMS WERE ORGANIZED

The contemporary church uses many terms to describe its lay
leaders, including "deacon board," "elder board," "church
board," "ruling elders," "board of trustee" and "board of control." The selection process for lay leaders is also accomplished
in many different ways, depending on a church's official rules,
theological roots, denominational traditions and personal preferences. Interestingly, the Early Church also had an assortment
of titles and selection strategies for its leaders.

At the start, the apostles were the Church's only leaders.
They had been eyewitnesses at the Cross and at the empty
tomb. What better training could a leadership team member
have? However, as the Twelve aged and the Early Church grew,
that requirement for leadership could not be maintained.
Thus, as Christianity marched across the book of Acts, the
emerging Church frequently refined its organizational patterns as a way to increase efficiency. The biblical record indi-
cates that they felt free to use any organization pattern that
seemed useful.

For example, the Early Church nominated leaders and drew
straws to decide who would replace the traitor, Judas. Peter led
the discussion.

> "Judas must now be replaced. The replacement must
> come from the company of men who stayed together
> with us from the time Jesus was baptized by John up to
> the day of his ascension, designated along with us as a
> witness to his resurrection."

They nominated two: Joseph Barsabbas, nicknamed Justus, and Matthias. Then they prayed, "You, oh God, know every one of us inside and out. Make plain which of these two men you choose to take the place in this ministry and leadership that Judas threw away in order to go his own way." They then drew straws. Matthias won, and was counted in with the eleven apostles (Acts 1:20-26, *THE MESSAGE*).

The next organizational meeting was convened to elect the Church's first official lay leadership group. The Twelve called for their election in Acts 6 at a time when "the disciples were increasing in numbers by leaps and bounds" (v. 1, *THE MESSAGE*). Although no actual attendance statistic is given, the *King James Version* calls the group of lay leaders a "multitude," the *New International Version* calls it the "group" and *THE MESSAGE* calls it "a congregation" (v. 5). Apparently the whole body of believers was involved in choosing the seven in Acts 6.

The organizational patterns of the Early Church were fluid as it grew from 12 to 120 to thousands of new believers.

IRREDUCIBLE REQUIREMENTS FOR LAY LEADERS

Although the organizational patterns changed frequently, members of the Early Church always had a soul longing to be led by godly people. Notice how this desire shines through Peter's charge in Acts 1:21-22, as the group considered a successor for Judas:

Therefore it is necessary to choose one of the men who have been with us the whole time the Lord Jesus went in and out among us, beginning from John's baptism to the time when Jesus was taken up from us. For one of these must become a witness with us of his resurrection.

In Acts 6, the Church chose lay leaders who exhibited spiritual strengths. Their clergy leaders advised them to "choose seven men from among you whom everyone trusts, men full of the Holy Spirit and good sense, and we'll assign them this task" (vv. 3-4, *THE MESSAGE*). A fourth characteristic came into play when Stephen was described as "a man full of *faith*" (v. 5, *THE MESSAGE*, emphasis added).

The four-part checklist of qualities they developed is as valid for selecting leaders today as it was in the Early Church. What a list: common sense, a solid reputation, a life of faith and dependence upon the Spirit.

Amazing results followed their election to places of trust. The record shows "the Word of God prospered. The number of disciples in Jerusalem increased dramatically. Not least, a great many priests submitted themselves to the faith" (Acts 6:8, *THE MESSAGE*). Although no further word is recorded about five of them, two from that group changed the world forever. The biblical account crackles with emotion: "Stephen [one of the two], brimming with God's grace and energy, was doing wonderful things among the people, unmistakable signs that God was among them" (Acts 6:9, *THE MESSAGE*).

Stephen became the first Christian martyr—serious stuff. Beyond the impact of Stephen's death was his legacy of evangelism. One of his converts was a man named Saul of Tarsus. Better known as Paul, he turned the world upside down, and his impact is still felt to this day.

Philip, who had the same ordinary job as Stephen, fled persecution. In Samaria, he instinctively shared the gospel with a people group hated by the Jews.

A red-hot revival broke out. The news scandalized leaders in Jerusalem—how could God be using a layman like this? They sent Peter and John to investigate. Soon after they arrived, they became convinced that this revival was the real thing, because so many lives had been transformed.

After that, as if layman Philip had not already been stretched enough, God sent him to win an Ethiopian eunuch, the first African convert (see Acts 6—8).

Stephen and Philip were elected to do ordinary tasks, but they became key players in the missionary movement of the Early Church, introducing the gospel to two new people groups.

LESSONS FOR TODAY

Today, many congregations act as if they are choosing a corporate board of directors rather than a team of spiritual leaders. A new pastor or team leader is selected for what he knows, who he

Many congregations act as if they are choosing a corporate board of directors rather than a team of spiritual leaders.

knows or what he owns rather than who he is or who he can become. Then he leads a church or team as if it were a business rather than an intimate branch of the family of God. He turns a church into a human organization instead of a holy organism and makes the church into a bottom-line corporation instead of a frontline faith army. Consequently, the church becomes more of a well-oiled organizational machine than a rescue station for drowning sinners. In this sad condition, the church may have money, capable personnel and secular savvy, but it lacks passion and risk-taking faith for the work of our Lord.

These are precise reasons why lay leaders need a close connection to Jesus. Such a relationship provides a holy energy and creativity that leaders of secular organizations do not have. Personal transformation is the most essential of all leadership qualifications.

Check out those whom Jesus called to be part of the original Twelve. They were ordinary men. But notice how Jesus shaped their perspectives and stretched their souls for effective service. He talked with them, prayed with them, affirmed them, warned them and challenged them. He stretched them and cared for them. The secret of their effectiveness was their close tie to Jesus.

Although writers and preachers enjoy emphasizing how Jesus empowered ordinary disciples to do great things for Him, another factor must be considered: Their relationships made them better people. Serving on a church decision-making team has been known to radically change a person:

- from complainer to contributor,
- from taker to giver,
- from adversary to partner,
- from selfish to generous,
- from suspicious to trusting,
- from useless to integral,
- from spectator to servant,
- from whiner to affirmer,
- from spectator to team player.

WHY A TEAM OF LAY LEADERS?

There are many good reasons for working in teams at church. Gene Wilkes in *Jesus on Leadership* and Elaine Biech in *Successful Team Building Tools* help us develop the following list of advantages of working in teams in a church:

1. Teams provide increased input that helps the group develop better ideas and make better decisions.
2. Teams provide higher quality output.
3. Teams involve everyone in the process.
4. Teams encourage a sense of community by sharing credit for both victories and defeats.
5. Teams are more likely to implement plans because leader and group members consider themselves accountable to each other.
6. Teams demonstrate the synergism principal whereby two can do more than twice what one can do.
7. Teams are how Jesus did ministry.
8. Teams increase opportunities to draw on an individual's strengths and to compensate for his weaknesses.
9. Teams develop a sense of togetherness, a feeling of belonging, so it is easier for members to build strong personal relationships.[1]

HOW JESUS DEVELOPED HIS TEAM

The essential requirement for being on the first team of disciples was to be an authentic follower of Jesus. Our Lord appealed to the inner longing God created in every human being—the desire to make life count. He called the disciples to follow Him. As they responded to that call, He shaped their individual talents, backgrounds and experiences into a force for the gospel.

Jesus stretched them spiritually and used their human talents. But He did more: He also helped get them ready for the unbelievable demands they would face once He was gone. He taught them who they were and gave them vision of what they could become. He even made the amazing promise they would do greater things than He had done. This promise, which is still good today, should be enough to get every believer to immediately sign up for Christian service.

Basketball coach Pat Riley was probably not thinking about signing up for a church decision-making team, yet his words underscore a reality for church leaders: "You must give up something in the immediate present, comfort, ease, recognition, quick rewards to attract something even better in the future: a full heart and sense that you did something which counted. Without that sacrifice, you'll never know your team's potential, or your own."[2]

Riley's words sound like something Jesus might have said. Here is how He did it:

1. He Chose Diversity to Strengthen His Team

He loved bringing people with radically different backgrounds together. Look at the list: Peter was a hot reactor, a talk-before-you-think character; John had a burn-up-the-village personality but was later called the beloved; Matthew was a tax collector; Luke was a physician; Thomas was called the doubter; and Andrew showed the traits of a live-out-of-the-limelight personal evangelist.

Perhaps these differences were part of our Lord's strategy to help the Early Church and us realize that every leadership team needs to include people of many different abilities and backgrounds. It could be that the Owner of the Team called the Early

Church to be a macrocosm of what the Church is to be in every age: inclusive, accepting and uniquely gifted.

On a related point, the 10-day waiting period in the Upper Room may have been necessary simply because it took that long for them to allow the Spirit to unite them for their Kingdom task in spite of their differences.

2. He Trained the Team As They Served

Notice the way Jesus trained His disciples as they served together. Meal after meal, He discussed spiritual issues with them. As they walked together, He taught them. Their priorities turned from trying to be special to serving the needy as they watched Him feed the hungry and heal the sick.

An example of an unexpected teaching moment was when Jesus multiplied the lad's meager lunch. He used that event to teach His disciples about extravagant Kingdom resources (see John 6:1-15).

On another occasion, Jesus' conversation with the oft-married woman at the well taught the disciples to reexamine their own highly developed prejudices (see John 4:1-26). And, of course, Jesus' visit to Lazarus's home after His friend had died taught His disciples new lessons about life, death and servanthood (see John 11:1-44).

3. He Unfolded a God-Sized Mission

The concept was radical and visionary. An itinerant teacher challenged ordinary disciples to win the world. Sometimes Jesus' followers must have turned to each other and said, "Does He know who we are? He must be exaggerating! No one has ever won the entire world."

Although there were only 11 disciples after the defection of Judas, their Master gave them the big task of reaching the entire planet. With that assignment, He promised to empower them and to be with them even unto the end of the age (see Matt. 28:18-20). Eleven plus the One made them so invincible that the world has not been the same since.

> *He gave the disciples a task so great it required their best plus total dependence upon God.*

This is our Lord's pattern. He gave the disciples a task so great that it required their best plus total dependence upon God. Of course, when this happens, the glory for achievement is wholly His, but it is achievement. The personal serendipity is that disciples develop spiritually as His divine empowerment works through them.

4. He Demonstrated the Power of Love in Building Team Relationships

In the kingdom of Christ, most issues revolve around human relationships. Check out the Gospels and notice how the first disciples were often almost forced to apply the gospel to those with whom they came into contact each day. Learning to love God and each other was a significant part of the conditioning process Jesus put His team through, because He knew that so much of their future effectiveness required them to be loving disciples of the Lord.

He taught them that love is the main ingredient of everything the church does. Love is the way leaders connect people to the Lord. Seldom do people come into the fellowship of the church because they are bossed in, pushed in, tricked in or slicked in. The majority are loved into the church.

5. He Trained His Team Through Adversity

The Twelve were stretched through personal relationships, confrontation, trying conditions and outright persecution (as we have already noted). In each situation, Jesus had a lesson for His disciples and He was there to provide the strength to get them through. These common experiences helped the disciples be molded into an achieving team.

Placid days with no rain, wind, thunder or lightning are nice if you are a weatherman or beach bum. But if you are a Christian, real growth, as the disciples soon experienced, usually comes through the storms, floods and fires of life. Our Lord knows this and He is always trying to help His followers grow great souls as part of becoming effective leaders in His Church. To be given a leadership assignment in the Church is to be given an opportunity to grow.

6. He Showed the Way to Greatness

Jesus' blueprint is clear: Servanthood is the path to greatness. As the disciples looked back at the earthly life of their Lord through the perspective of the Cross, their memories must have blushed with shame as they remembered their silly bids for power. They learned, and so must we, that the question "Who will be greatest?" has no place in the divine plan. Service and the giving of one's life for the Kingdom are Jesus' recipe for satisfaction. The who-is-the-greatest issue does not seem to matter much after a person gives her life to the gospel.

The mature Peter understood how real greatness was achieved and how it felt. Read what he wrote to church leaders: "So be content with who you are, and don't put on airs. God's strong hand is on you; he'll promote you at the right time. Live carefree before God; he is most careful with you" (1 Pet. 5:6-7, *THE MESSAGE*).

7. He Trusted His Followers with His Kingdom

What a huge risk Jesus took when He entrusted His kingdom to the disciples. Their loyalty, dependability and follow-through had not been impressive. Their understanding of what mattered was mixed at best. They had been with Jesus for only three years, but He still trusted them with what mattered most to Him.

As this example shows, Jesus often used a basic principle of coach-to-player development. The principle is simple to express but sometimes difficult to implement. Don Shula and Ken Blanchard, in their book *The Little Book of Coaching*, explain the idea well:

> Who believes in you? . . . That person's vision of what you were capable of ignited something inside you. You said to yourself, "Well if they think I can do it, maybe I can." You were challenged to reach down into yourself and call forth the effort that matched their vision of your potential. Lo and behold, you rose to it.[3]

Christians, when trusted with important responsibilities, often stretch to do their best and depend on the Holy Spirit for the rest. In such a partnership they achieve effectiveness—sometimes they even reach greatness.

A beautiful illustration of this appears in the Acts 4 account of how God used Peter and John to heal a crippled man. The event caused consternation among the religious intelligentsia who wanted a meeting of religious professional leaders to be called. Rulers, religious leaders, religion scholars—almost everybody showed up. The Bible reports what happened:

> They [the religious leaders] couldn't take their eyes off them—Peter and John standing there so confident, so sure of themselves! Their fascination deepened when

they realized these two were laymen with no training in Scripture or formal education. They recognized them as companions of Jesus, but with the man right before them, seeing him standing there so upright—so healed!—what could they say against that? (Acts 4:13-15, *THE MESSAGE*).

Perhaps a branch office of a "what could they say against that" group is needed in every contemporary congregation to help convince those outside the church that our Lord's team is really in partnership with Omnipotence. The key sentence in Acts tells it all: "Their fascination deepened when they realized these two were laymen with no training in Scripture or formal education." This observation, of course, was true but remember that the disciples had been trained by being with Jesus and watching Him do His ministry.

Jesus saw His disciples for what they could become rather than what they were. And He sees us like that, too. Because He sees our potential, He trusts the future of His Kingdom to us.

8. Jesus Pointed Toward His Priorities

Sometimes when reading the Scriptures, we might conclude that every day with Jesus was a special event or a parable. Certainly studying under the Savior's tutelage was intense, challenging and satisfying, but it did not mean everyday life was suspended. The disciples still had to eat, take out the trash and pay their taxes. So it was not unusual for Jesus to send His disciples ahead of time to the next town to arrange for housing, food and supplies. But He always wanted them to understand that there was more to what He was about than logistics and material items. He wanted them to know that His purpose was to transform people from their sinful pasts and give them new beginnings.

The lesson contemporary lay leaders can learn from the way Jesus did His work is that the church must be focused on lofty purposes, not just mere survival. Leaders must pay attention to logistics. Buildings have to be financed, built and maintained. Budgets must be developed, funded and followed. But each of these activities must be kept in perspective and must contribute to God's big, eternal purposes.

When team members move in this direction, the church, in her most effective hour, actually becomes a mission station providentially placed in a particular location as an outpost to serve needy people. In such a setting, congregational leaders become missionaries who win people to Christ. The redemption of people to new life in Christ is why the Church exists. Surprisingly, survival becomes almost automatic when lay leaders make sure that the main thing is the main thing.

9. Jesus Called His Followers to Be Worldly Separatists

"Worldly separatist" sounds like an oxymoron, yet Christians are to be immersed in the world but not of it. That is precisely the way Jesus prayed for the disciples: "My prayer is not that you take them out of the world but that you protect them from the evil one" (John 17:15).

Apparently our Lord meant for His disciples and for us to be detached in spirit from the world. That does not mean He plans to take us out of the world. Neither does it mean that any of us should stop being salt in the world.

It does mean, however, that Jesus wanted the spirit of the world taken out of His followers, and that includes each of us. Paul described it this way: "Therefore come out from them and be separate, says the Lord. Touch no unclean thing, and I will receive you" (2 Cor. 6:17).

Jesus once prayed, "I will remain in the world no longer, but they are still in the world, and I am coming to you. Holy Father, protect them by the power of your name—the name you gave me—so that they may be one as we are one" (John 17:11).

Our Lord's teaching is clear: We are to keep spiritually fit and faithful *in the world.*

10. Jesus Taught the Power of a Great Purpose

Look back over the development of your own spiritual life, and you will discover that you grew the most at those times when your work for Christ stretched your limits.

This introduces a seldom-discussed principle: Great causes develop strong Christians. When a person gives himself to a great cause, it often does more for the individual than the individual does for the cause. Service done for the Lord Jesus blesses the person who serves fully as much as the person who receives the service. The person who gives a cup of cold water is as blessed as the thirsty person who receives it.

Efforts to build God's kingdom develop spiritual sinew and steadfastness. Often service done in the name of Jesus is a magnificent gift God gives us to catapult us beyond an ordinary 9-to-5 existence. Sacrificial efforts for missions are good for the giver. Serving the needs of the poor makes the one who serves stronger and spiritually richer. Looking into the faces of the destitute and dying, as Mother Teresa loved to point out, is where we see the face of Jesus.

11. Jesus Gave Meaning to Life

After people in Western societies have their food, shelter and clothing needs met, they want to know if their lives have meaning, if they count for something, if living is worthwhile. Researchers Richard Leider and David Shapiro conclude, "Having lived a meaningless life is the one deadly fear of most people."[4]

Jesus answered the meaning question with a concise, clear 14-word summary: "I have come that they many have life, and have it to the full." (John 10:10). As He developed His disciples into authentic, wholesome Christians, He was preparing them to play on a win-the-world team. He showed them *agape* love. He gave each of them opportunities to grow, to test their talents, to succeed, to make mistakes and even to embarrass themselves. He seemed willing to do anything to help them become all they could be. But our Lord's development of the disciples was not to merely give them warm and fuzzy relationships but also to make them stalwart Kingdom leaders. He needed them to carry on His work in the world. And that is what they did, largely because of what they learned while being with Him. Go back to Scripture and observe the disciples in the maturity of their years; you will find them fulfilling the purposes of Christ in the details of their lives.

The lesson for today is that clergy and lay leaders do not fulfill the purpose God has for them by attending meetings, participating in happy collaborations of ideas, keeping members of the group content or even bringing the coffee and donuts. To be a member of a church decision-making group is to commit to do something significant for Christ. To put it concisely, our development as disciples is to get us ready for action and achievement.

NURTURING MEMBERS OF THE TEAM CHRIST HAS GIVEN YOU

The plan and pattern of Scripture never set out to build great churches but to build great Christians who in turn build great churches. New Testament scholar William Barclay summarizes Paul's doctrine of the Church like this:

> The church is the company of men and women who have dedicated their lives to Christ, whose relationship to

Christ is as close as that of husband and of wife, whose relationship to each other is as firm as the stones within a building, and whose supreme glory is that they are the Body in whom Christ dwells, and through which He acts upon the world.[5]

Jesus' way connects people with the love of God and then encourages them to live out its implications in relationship with others.

This nurturing relationship flourishes best when the lay and clergy leaders of a church see themselves as a microcosm of what they believe the Body of Christ should be. Remember, as a church leader, you ultimately do not work with things but with people. Things are to be used, but people are to be cherished because the Savior came for each one of us. An authentic Christian leader loves people more than he loves his position or prominence.

The lyrics of "The Servant Song" help us sing this big idea into our souls:

Brother (and sister) let me be your servant,
Let me be as Christ to you;
Pray that I may have the grace to
Let you be my servant, too.
We are pilgrims on a journey;
We are brothers (and sisters) on the road.
We are here to help each other
Walk the mile and bear the load.[6]

Notes

1. Elaine Biech, *The Pfeiffer Book of Successful Team Building Tools* (San Francisco, CA: Jossey-Bass/Pfeiffer, 2001), p. 2; and Gene Wilkes, *Jesus on Leadership* (Wheaton, IL: Tyndale House, 1998), p. 213.

2. Pat Riley, *The Winner Within* (New York: Putnam, 1993), p. 53.

3. Ken Blanchard and Don Shula, *The Little Book of Coaching* (New York: Harper, 2001), p. 11.

4. Richard Leider and David Shapiro, quoted in Laurie Beth Jones, *The Path* (New York: Hyperion Books, 1996), p. X.

5. William Barclay, *The Mind of St. Paul* (New York: Harper and Brothers, 1958), p. 256.

6. *Sing to the Lord* (Kansas City, MO: Lillenas Publishing Company, 1993), p. 679.

The laity, on the whole, have been in the stands as spectators, and the clergy have been on the field playing the game. . . . The laity must come out of the stands as spectators and take the field as players; and the clergymen must come off the field as players and take the sidelines as coaches of a team.

E. STANLEY JONES, *SAYINGS OF E. STANLEY JONES*

CHAPTER 4

SEVEN HABITS OF HIGHLY EFFECTIVE LAY LEADERS

AN INCREDIBLE JOURNEY AWAITS THOSE WHO MASTER THE LESSONS

Look into the deep places of my soul, Lord Jesus,
Cleanse me from lust for status and love of power.
Make my service to Your Church blameless and
productive.
Shape my motives and actions into authentic
Christlikeness.
Make me a lovable servant and a pleasing hired
hand for You.
I want the love of Christ to radiate through my
life.
Amen.

As children, most of us played Pin the Tail on the Donkey. Today the game has regained its popularity in many contemporary congregations but with a new twist. Unwittingly, as if blindfolded, clergy and lay leaders alike sometimes pin a potpourri of criticism on their churches. We ourselves, as lay leaders and clergy, must first become individually what we dream of the church becoming collectively. The church must be "us," never "them," if it is ever to become our favorite. No church can become more than its leaders are or are willing to become.

To increase the church's impact and multiply its effectiveness, renewal must start in congregations we serve and with individual believers like us.

There is a sign of hope. Increasingly, lay leaders of congregations seem eager to see the work of Christ reenergized in the churches that they lead. Such a trend must be fanned into a holy flame that moves from abstract notions about revival to a concrete reality of authentic, radical, do-or-die, sold-out-for-Christ commitments. In the wake of the September 11 terrorist attacks, the world may be more ready for renewal than at any other time in modern history.

Ecclesiastical governing bodies cannot make this happen—too many people believe what these groups decree makes no difference in individual congregations. An insightful lay leader observed to a reporter in the hall outside a denominational legislative conference, "They don't do anything that makes any difference to the congregation I'm a part of, so we don't care what they say. And if we don't care, then certainly the world doesn't care."

It is a lot like what a newspaper reporter observed: "The pope is the darling of the masses, but few people pay much attention to what he says."

At the same time, it is obvious that people who order their lives according to contemporary secular values cannot renew themselves, even when they feel morally bankrupt and spiritually shallow. Therefore, if moral and spiritual renewal is to come, it must start with leaders in local congregations. To renew the church and our society, lay leaders and clergy must become more spiritually authentic, biblically faithful and passionately aggressive for the Kingdom.

As lay leaders fill this renewal gap in local congregations, a dynamic climate of growing ministry will result. To make this a reality, individuals who influence and shape congregations must be absolutely honest in their assessments of their churches.

They must see what is broken and repair it, or what is rusty and replace it. Since each congregation has its own attitudes, atmosphere and priorities, it usually requires someone within the group to start change in a church. Thus, improvement or renewal most often comes from one individual's influence more than from any committee decision.

Although conventional wisdom says one bad apple spoils a bushel, in the church a little salt preserves the whole. One person, plus Jesus, is enough to start renewal. In fact, the church survives and thrives by living out the salty teachings of Jesus. Though you may question whether a single individual can spark renewal in an entire congregation, the answer is yes.

Since a congregation is the sum total of its members' commitments and attitudes, it logically follows that each lay leader has the incredible influence to make a church better, nobler and stronger. A healthy, nurturing environment can be started by one courageous believer—try it!

There is a church not far from where I (Neil) live that has been battered for years by one aggressive, controlling man. Almost single-handedly, he caused three pastors to leave the church and to leave ministry, altogether. Lay people in the church warned their pastors to not pay so much attention to that one person, but every pastor did.

One key lay leader complained, "Pastors shouldn't let one negative, complaining person affect them." But controllers and complainers always impact ministers. Ignoring the immobilizing power of negativism is never easy.

Are controllers and complainers undermining the work of the gospel in your church? If they are, then why not become a Christ-motivated, revolutionary-change agent who intervenes before your pastor checks out? Consider how you can counter-act and eliminate difficulties. Ask yourself what you can do to make your church more Christlike. Ask yourself what you can do to make your church your pastor's favorite.

> *As you form a strategy, remember that a minister finds his or her greatest satisfaction in building up people spiritually.*

As you form a strategy, remember that a minister finds his greatest satisfaction in building up people spiritually. Nothing brings a faithful pastor greater fulfillment than knowing lay leaders are growing in their relationship with Jesus Christ and together helping develop the congregation into a genuine New Testament church.

Have you ever thought about how being a great marriage partner is a great gift you give to your spouse, and it also enriches your own life? In a similar way, when you become an authentic Christian-change agent, you give your church a magnificent gift that also enriches you. This way everyone wins. You delight your pastor's heart. You impact others with Christ's love, and the Christlike atmosphere of the church shows that controllers are counterfeit Christians. In this effort you undermine the influence of people who would wound the congregation. And you strengthen your walk with God. Your attitude, your commitment to Christ and the joy of your faith help shape your church, edify the congregation and allow your pastor to enjoy the excitement of seeing people develop spiritually.

Every pastor dreams of leading a congregation like the church Luke described in Acts 2:

> All the believers lived in a wonderful harmony, holding everything in common. They sold whatever they owned and pooled their resources so that each person's need was met.
>
> They followed a daily discipline of worship in the Temple followed by meals at home, every meal a celebration, exuberant and joyful, as they praised God. People in general liked what they saw. Every day their number grew as God added those who were saved (vv. 44-47, *THE MESSAGE*).

With the goal of personally becoming a significant part of your favorite church, let's consider seven habits that make lay leaders effective in the church, while increasing their satisfaction with the journey.

HABIT #1: START WITH THE BASICS

Luke describes the Early Church as a congregation in which members were devoted to Christ, to the apostles' teaching, to fellowship and to the breaking of bread (see Acts 2:42). The devotion of these believers gave them a winsome attractiveness that drew others to them. This always happens. Genuine commitment to Christ attracts people, even when they do not understand the magnetism. The drawing power is a believer's whole-hearted devotion to the Savior.

Such commitment charms and delights those who observe it. Such devotion enriches the life of the one who stretches himself to make the commitment, even as it attracts others to the Lord. Veteran pastor and United States Senate Chaplain Lloyd J. Ogilvie explains this attraction in a one-sentence description of the first-century church: "People wanted to be with those contagious, praising Christians and have what the Spirit had given them."[1]

These observations about the power of commitment lead to a sobering question every church leader must ask himself: *Does my walk with Christ make anyone want to know Him?* Every congregation needs lay leaders who refuse to be distant, cold disciples of Jesus. This is an essential issue. Every clergy member and lay leader must abandon unlovely harshness to become warm, compassionate imitators of Christ, who love the people He loves. Conversely, attempting Christian leadership without an authentic relationship to our Lord produces the worst kind of loneliness, creates inner emptiness and ultimately repels people who have not made up their minds about Christ.

You may feel that you already have an intimate walk with God, or you may know that you have not arrived. Either way, it is wise to dig into your own spiritual depths and examine what you find. A good place to start is to apply this poem by Dom Helder Camara to your own spiritual development:

> The noise
> that prevents us hearing
> the voice of God
> is not,
> is truly not,
> the clamour of man,

the racket of cities,
still less
the stirring of the wind
or the whispering of water.
The noise
that completely smothers
the voice of God
is the inner uproar
of outrageous self-esteem,
of awakening suspicion,
of unsleeping ambition.[2]

HABIT #2: APPLY JESUS' PERSPECTIVE TO CHURCH POLITICS

A veteran minister once observed, "Wherever two or more people live or work together, you have politics." How true this is—politics thrives everywhere, even in the Church.

By politics, we mean maneuvering, manipulating, positioning or acting upon an agenda in a manner that benefits an individual in a self-centered or destructive way and is evidenced by the misuse of power, authority, position or opportunity.

We are not referring to going to the church potluck because everyone else will be there, avoiding orange ink when printing the church newsletter because you know the pastor hates the color or recommending a friend be hired as the church secretary. These acts may be common courtesies, wise and even useful. However, Christians fall into destructive, controlling politics when they strike deals, trade advantages, grasp control and posture themselves for advancement. The church and its leaders get caught in spiritual dead-end streets when they think this kind of behavior is God's will.

This kind of raw politics knows no bounds. It crosses generations, denominations and geographical borders. It even infects people who were idealistic when they started their walks with the Lord. How frightening it is to watch as certain individuals become more adept at politicking as they get seniority in the church.

The holy work of the church will improve measurably if you admit politics exists but refuse to play the manipulation game.

The more politics in a church, the more problems it has. For example, membership in the "in-group" often becomes more important than accomplishing Christ's mission in the world. This is a destructive trap that often snares church leaders and easily grinds the real work of the church to a snail's pace or an outright standstill. Why? This happens because more and more energy and funds are directed toward taking care of "important" people, rather than Christ's mission.

It is difficult to correct such a situation, but it must be done. One person can do a lot to start church renewal simply by confronting corrupt behavior and challenging people with a call to mission. Meanwhile, you must apply Jesus' principles to your own attitudes and actions to be sure that you are not part of the problem.

The holy work of the church will improve measurably if you admit politics exists but refuse to play the manipulation game.

Beware of church politics—it can become a fatal, faith-destroying disease that often starts with a tiny infection or a minor accommodation. This means every leader must examine her conduct in light of Jesus' teachings concerning genuine greatness. Our Lord taught and demonstrated by His life that servanthood was the path to greatness. Some of His servanthood symbols were a basin, a towel and the dirty feet of his followers.

The spirit of Jesus can revolutionize our service in the church if certain corrections are made.

Evaluate Personal Motives

Thoroughly examine the driving force behind your actions and what you hope to gain. If you are being considered for a high-profile assignment in the church, ask yourself why you want the position. Is your purpose to accomplish Christ's mission or to gratify your ego? You know the answer; so does God.

Trust God

Believe God when He promises that He will work in every area of your life. He can be expected to overrule even the most blatant, manipulative orchestration of self-centered, crafty church politicians.

Be Christlike

Cultivate personal piety so that your character is attractive, sought after and needed by the congregation. Refuse to play the political game, but be willing to serve when opportunities are presented.

Reform the System

When you gain status by serving with distinction, use the platform you have attained to reform the church from within. Some of the saddest people are those who preside over structures they once scorned but fail to make any significant changes. Try to be like Abraham Lincoln, who vowed, if given an opportunity, he would stop slavery—he did not forget that vow when he became president. Ask yourself if you handle authority and politics in a way that pleases God.

Promote Compassion

The Church has a horrific history of wounding many of its members and those it tries to reach with the gospel.

Focus on the mission and, every time you get the opportunity, speak up for the real cause of Christ's Church. Self-interest and political efforts begin to fade when believers focus on the mission.

Remember Who You Were

If you gain political power, remember how misused authority frustrated you when you were one of the "little people." Refuse to fool yourself into believing political half-truths about yourself and others. Do not make a speech that others could interpret as meaning, *It's God's will since it seems so good to me.*

Check Your Competence

If you are asked to serve in a position for which you have no skills or experience, decline the offer. Suspect your motives or the processes of a system that give you an opportunity for which you have no gifts, skills and previous interest. If you find you have a task for which you do not have skills and cannot acquire them, resign, get the task reassigned or humble yourself by asking for adequate help. In any organization, especially the church, persons placed in assignments beyond their competency destroy morale and retard achievement. It is a vivid illustration of the secular Peter Principle of being promoted beyond one's competence, just dressed in Sunday duds.

HABIT #3: TALK HEALTHY TALK

Every church has a communication grapevine because Christians, like all other humans, love to talk. You are part of the grapevine whether you know it or not. People often ask probing questions of those who know information so that they can pass on what they gather. Then a kernel of truth gets exaggerated. Church rumors usually focus on highly visible people such as the pastor and those close to him or her. Informers often use loose talk to put themselves in the spotlight. In most grapevine discussions, accuracy is compromised simply because the talker seldom knows all of the facts.

When inaccurate information is passed from person to person, it causes lots of mischief for innocent parties. Deception and false conclusions plant seeds of confusion, distrust and doubt—all destructive viruses in any church.

Gossip can easily destroy a church's mission—and it often does. It encourages insensitivity to others; prejudges situations, persons and causes; and encourages everyone to express radical, or even un-Christian, opinions. Scripture explains the problems corrupt communication creates:

A word out of your mouth may seem of no account, but it can accomplish nearly anything—or destroy it!

It only takes a spark, remember, to set off a forest fire. A careless or wrongly placed word out of your mouth can do that. By our speech we can ruin the world, turn harmony to chaos, throw mud on a reputation, send the whole world up in smoke and go up in smoke with it, smoke right from the pit of hell.

. . . With our tongues we bless God our Father; with the same tongues we curse the very men and women he made in his image. Curses and blessings out of the same mouth! (Jas. 3:6-10, *THE MESSAGE*).

Use the Grapevine

One way to be certain that rumors do not ruin a church is to use the grapevine as an information network to "gossip" about good news concerning the church.

Begin to transform the grapevine into a positive forum by asking why church people talk so much. They may be intensely interested but lack information; therefore, they converse to find out if others know more than they do. If this idea has validity, why not provide talkers with more information as a starting point for using the grapevine to bless the church? For example, one recreational talker questions leaders in different settings and at different times; then like a private investigator, he adds up the details and becomes the resident informant who spreads the story. When you see this pattern, give the self-appointed investigator the information you want known. Then, let him talk.

Why not think of ways to make your church's grapevine useful? Why not put significant facts on the grapevine? It is wonderful fun to tell a positive story to a talker and then wait to see how long it takes the information to get back to you and to hear what embellishments have been attached along the way. Sometimes the resident talker forgets who told her the story and repeats it to the originator. Sometimes the tale comes back in hours, but it almost always comes back within a few days.

Since people are bound to talk, why not give them something positive to discuss? Putting accurate messages on the grapevine is easier than duplicating them on a copy machine, recording them on someone's answering machine or using e-mail.

Habit #4: Seek God's Direction

Scripture promises guidance for life and service. Yet few church decision-making groups diligently seek God's direction in the details of their efforts for God. When crunch time comes in congregational decisions, they tend to lean on their experience, logic, understanding or opinion. How soon we forget how many mistakes happen when we do what we want in the church and then call it God's will.

In so much of contemporary congregational life, an attitude prevails that everyone can express his or her opinion freely about anything, no matter how outrageous the position. Since democracy is so treasured in our civic life, we assume everyone has a right, according to the First Amendment, to speak his or her mind in church. The last word for the work of God, however, is not the prevailing group opinion or anyone's personal view but God's will. Human opinion and wisdom must be subservient.

Operating within this God-designed framework, every decision-making group must seek to understand what God thinks about an issue. Scripture provides abiding principles that can be applied to most situations. Divine guidance and the combined judgment of committed Christians help us find our way through complicated issues. The divine perspective can be made known to us through prayer, dialogue or even the study of Church history, particularly on issues where the Bible seems to be silent. Admittedly, finding the will of God is sometimes difficult, but seeking such direction always helps a decision-making group remember who owns the church.

Ministry becomes much more difficult, however, when church decision-making groups do not even try to find the will of God. This can happen with any group in any church. Team members express their opinions or prejudices, a vote is taken, the majority rules, and the group moves on to the next item on the agenda. When you make decisions this way, you may falsely assume that the Lord's purpose for His Church is the prevailing opinion of the voting team members. However, God sometimes surprises His followers by siding with the thoughtful minority. At other times, He has something in mind that is completely different from any human proposal.

Every clergyman and lay church leader remembers politically charged occasions in their churches when decisions were made in haste. God was not consulted with even one short prayer; there was no search of Scripture; and no one attempted to hush noisy personal opinions so that God's directive could be heard. Often those events are later justified by calling them the will of God. Shamefully, some outcomes are so disastrous that it is laughable to blame God. One writer suggests calling our judgments God's will is the same as taking His name in vain.

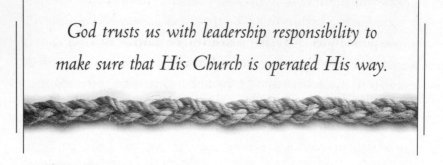

God trusts us with leadership responsibility to make sure that His Church is operated His way.

Can anyone seriously believe God is pleased with congregational and denominational decision-making groups that operate His Church according to their own designs?

Perhaps every church should require that decisions only be made after an honest effort has been made to find the mind of the Lord. The Bible supports this approach:

> Real wisdom, God's wisdom, begins with a holy life and is characterized by getting along with others. It is gentle and reasonable, overflowing with mercy and blessings, not hot one day and cold the next, not two-faced. You can

develop a healthy, robust community that lives right with God and enjoy its results *only* if you do the hard work of getting along with each other, treating each other with dignity and honor (Jas. 3:17-18, *THE MESSAGE*).

God trusts us with leadership responsibility to make sure that His Church is operated His way, and He expects to see the details worked out at a local level. In *Pot-Shots at the Preacher*, James Sparks reminds us of the risks God takes when He entrusts His Church to the likes of us:

The care and feeding of congregations is truly a testimony to the mystery of God's ways as well as His sense of humor. Throughout the ages, He has gathered His people into communities of faith and given them full responsibility for the treasures of faith. That God should choose to do this through congregations, so diverse and sometimes capricious, is a witness to His patience, love and utter trust in humankind in spite of our inherent foibles.[3]

The bottom line of seeking and following the guidance of the Lord for His Church is that He is ready to help us find our way if we earnestly seek His will. Why try to make it without His help?

HABIT #5: REAP THE PERSONAL HARVEST OF SPIRITUAL GROWTH

Authentic congregational leadership starts and continues with an individual who cultivates a growing, personal relationship with Christ. In business and government, leaders are appointed or elected on the basis of their training, experience, prestige, financial clout or connections. But leadership in the work of God, from biblical times until now, requires stalwart Christian character as a bedrock foundation. Acts 6 records how the Early Church organized itself for greater efficiency by choosing leaders who demonstrated their faith and their wisdom and were full of the Holy Spirit. No mention was made of experience, brilliance, prestige or standing in the community, but following their election to church leadership, they quickly found themselves at the front lines of the spiritual battles of their time. Stephen was even stoned to death.

To keep growing spiritually is to acknowledge that the foundation for all service in the Kingdom is a vital relationship with Christ. That means we have met Him in a life-transforming encounter and continue to live in vital relationship with Him and His people. We keep our souls robust through worship, prayer and application of Scripture. We purposely choose to embody the examples of Christ in all we do and say. And we seek the mind of Christ in everything, specifically in decisions we help make for the church.

While this relationship qualifies a person for leadership, it also provides us with a satisfying quality of life. A wholehearted relationship with Christ, not just a mere cloak to make a leader appear pious, is the most essential ingredient for living a fulfilling life. Thus, none of us becomes a victorious Christian only as a means to become a leader—rather, every leader must first be an authentic Christian. Many people can lead secular organizations, but no one can effectively lead in a local congregation who does not have a personal relationship with Christ and continues to develop a Christlike character.

While on the surface this concept may sound like it restates an obvious fact about Christian life, in practice it shifts the focus of our leadership from doing to being, moves priority from the how of decision making to the why and transforms planning from the limitation of existing resources to finding miraculous ways of accomplishing a holy mission for God. Personal piety helps open a leader's vision to the holy work of the church.

Churches have their most significant impact on the world when they are led by people who are wholeheartedly devoted to Christ.

History tells us that churches have their most significant impact on the world when they are led by people who are wholeheartedly devoted to Christ. Such devotion starts and continues through a leader's relationship to Christ. Thus, the first query to a potential leader must be "Tell me how you met the Savior." The second question is closely related: "How have you grown in your relationship to Christ since you became a Christian?" A congregation cannot be an authentic Christ-centered church when led by people who are only qualified by their seniority, talent, money and social standing. Above all else, lay and clergy leaders in local congregations must know Christ.

HABIT #6: GROW PAST *THE PAST*

Recently I (Neil) renewed my friendship with a wonderful lay couple who has served Christ for nearly a half century. Wherever his company moved them, they have been at the forefront of a local congregation—always faithful, loyal and generous. When we reconnected, they informed me that they had changed denominations, because they were tired of years of disputes and conflicts in their previous church. They are not kooks, church hoppers or off-center church consumers; those who know them confirm that they have always been peacemakers. With a calm, steady influence, they have quieted murmurs and grievances in the churches where they served. But the accumulation of toxic relationships had taken its toll, and they felt the need for relief. Sadly, they likely will find similar situations in their new congregation and new denomination because such problems are pervasive in the contemporary church.

Anyone who has been around the Church for a while can identify with the seminary professor's description of contemporary congregations. He observed, "The church is a lot like Noah's ark. You couldn't stand the stench inside if you weren't afraid of the storms on the outside." We nod in sad agreement, because the Church we serve needs to become something more than it has been. Let's admit that many people have given up on the Church because it so often promises more than it delivers. It talks a holy game while being ruled by self-serving priorities. The Church of the future must become much more than it currently is.

Pastors and lay leaders must do what they can to make the Church nobler and more influential in our time. Meanwhile, as we work to make the Church better, we must find ways to rid ourselves of toxic thoughts and do away with past hurts. One old saint calls it relinquishment. We dare not allow past poisons to undermine the Church's present or abort its future. The way to free ourselves from these toxins is to apply Paul's advice to the Philippians to our own attitudes about the Church:

- Rejoice in the Lord always.
- Be gentle to all.

- Give up your fretful anxiety about everything, including the church.
- Allow God's peace to guard your hearts and minds.
- Dwell on the true, noble, right, pure, lovely and admirable.
- Reproduce in yourself what you have seen in spiritual giants (see Phil. 4:4-9).

An even stronger remedy for our toxins from the past shows up in the apostle's testimony:

> I consider everything a loss compared to the surpassing greatness of knowing Christ Jesus my Lord, for whose sake I have lost all things. I consider them rubbish, that I may gain Christ and be found in him, not having a righteousness of my own that comes from the law, but that which is through faith in Christ—the righteousness that comes from God and is by faith (Phil. 3:8-9).

HABIT #7: SEE YOUR CHURCH AS GOD SEES IT

Ask yourself, "What do I pretend not to see?" It is easy, while trying to be positive thinkers, to refuse to see ourselves, our families or our churches as they really are. By contrast, some people seem to have a need to see life, family and church in the worst possible light. Both extremes are harmful and must be avoided. We know that no human relationship is either ideal or totally flawed. It is human to try to ignore what is painful—our flaws. It is also natural to want to see only what is good and pleasurable and to, in our minds, elevate it to the status of perfection. Either way of thinking can fool us about the church and, thus, prevent the initiation of improvement.

How, then, should we realistically view the church? We should cherish its strengths. What makes your church strong? Is it the size of the congregation, the history, the building, the pastor, the location or the spiritually mature people who make up the core? How can these unique strengths be used to make the church even stronger? What does your church do better than other churches? What does your community think about your church's credibility?

Determine what changes are possible. Prioritize what needs to be done first. Then factor in what can be done with little effort and cost. For example, one church that meets in a multi-purpose room at a school dramatically increased its worship space by turning the movable seats in a different direction. It took 15 minutes to make a change that had a positive effect on every worshiper. It would have been foolish to put off such an uncomplicated modification just because funding prevented the church from building its own facility. Often a simple change helps church members see how they can consider making major changes. Do not refuse to do or postpone what *can* be done just because you cannot do everything immediately.

Test Your Reactions

When he was eight, one of my (Neil's) sons told me, "Whenever I ask you for something, you always answer no." As I thought about his reaction, I saw my son was right. Though my responses seemed grossly unfair to him, they were rooted in my Depression-era childhood. When I understood what made me respond the way I did, I tried to improve so that I could deal with issues more realistically. A similar change in outlook is needed in many churches. Ask yourself if you habitually respond to issues in particular ways and if any of those responses need to be modified.

Question your denials. Look for such phrases in your conversations as "I always say," "I don't do that," "I can't believe you said that," "If I were in their situation, I would never do that" or "I didn't say that or even think that." Each of these and similar phrases may be symptoms of unrealistic views about what is important to you. Any phrase you say that diverts responsibility to someone else or is slow to admit "it's me standing in the need of prayer" may be a denial of the truth.

We can fool ourselves so thoroughly and so frequently that we start to believe falsehoods about ourselves and about others. This happens when we take credit for what others do. It occurs when we are more interested in establishing blame than correcting difficulties. It may resurrect resentment from the past that will poison our present relationships and ministry efforts.

Forgiveness is usually taught and preached as being a Christian duty. But forgiveness can also be a gift that you give to yourself. Once you forgive yourself and forgive others, you can move on with your spiritual development without being locked in to past hurts.

The Bible charges us to forgive in the same measure that we have been forgiven. That is a lot. We forgive not only because God says that we should, but also because it makes us more whole as human beings and conserves our spiritual energy for what really matters.

OTHER HABITS GOD CAN USE

In listing these seven habits, there is always a danger of leaving out other significant characteristics. The habit that is overlooked may be the exact attribute you need to succeed as a Christian leader. Thus, it is important to go beyond a list of characteristics and get to the essential Christ-shaped personhood of an effective lay leader.

Why not take up the challenge to be the best leader you can be by being the best Christian you can be? This challenge is to *be* more like Christ before you attempt to *do* more for Him. Your congregation needs all the skills, strategies and solutions you can provide, but it needs your spirit, commitments and spiritual growth even more.

A Christ-saturated life, at its most fundamental level, is the most significant component of authentic Kingdom leadership. Well beyond elections, budgets and committee meetings is the impact your life makes. You can make a revolutionary spiritual difference in your congregation by living according to the mandates of Jesus and by counting service as the highest privilege of your life.

Be a leader God can use. Be a leader people gladly follow. Take your share of responsibility for the spiritual well-being of your church by allowing God to shape and stretch you closer to the image of Christ. Christlikeness creates incredible joy and draws others to Christ.

The Bible promises that God's power will work through us: "Now to Him who is able to do immeasurably more than all we ask or imagine, according to his power that is at work within us" (Eph. 3:20).

RENEWAL STRATEGIES FOR LAY LEADERS: EFFECTIVE LEADERS MUST BE GROWING CHRISTIANS

1. Draw close to Christ to reenergize your leadership motivations.
2. Renewal of a church is often rooted in the Christlike actions of its leaders.
3. Revival often starts in the heart of a church insider.
4. Refuse to allow negativism to strangle your church.
5. Apply the perspective of Jesus to church politics.

6. Refuse to glorify political manipulations by calling them the will of God.

7. Make positive use of the church grapevine.

8. Seek God's guidance in all church decisions.

9. Grow past the past.

10. Try to see your church as God sees it.

Notes

1. Lloyd J. Ogilvie, *The Commentator's Commentary*, vol. 5 (Waco, TX: Word, 1983), p. 75.

2. Dom Helder Camara, *A Thousand Reasons for Living* (Philadelphia: Fortress Press, 1981), p. 85.

3. James Allen Sparks, *Pot-Shots at the Preacher* (Nashville, TN: Abingdon Press, 1977), p. 97.

*The attitude Christ modeled for us is one that
should typify every Christian, whether in pulpit or pew,
whether leader of a vast organization or
solitary prayer warrior. Not puffed up with
self-importance, but poured out for others.*

CHARLES COLSON, *THE BODY*

CHAPTER 5

NEW TESTAMENT INSTRUCTIONS

WHAT THE PLAYBOOK REQUIRES OF THOSE WHO LEAD

Giver and Preserver of Holy Scripture,
I praise You for the written Word,
for its guidance for lay leaders,
for its instruction for pastors,
for its direction for our church.
Help every lay leader to see Your Church as a holy force for
righteousness in our world.
Help me see our church's potential as You see it.
Amen.

Before quarterback Kurt Warner and the St. Louis Rams took the field for Super Bowl XXXVI, they reviewed their playbook. They analyzed what works on the field and recapped what would be expected of each player. In the church, before we take the field in any ministry situation, whether it is a Super-Bowl caliber evangelistic crusade or an in-the-trenches, visit-the-members-in-the-hospital workout, we must review God's playbook: His Word.

No matter how well informed you are about lay leadership, it is essential to review what Scripture requires of us. The bottom line is that God uses people such as you and me to accomplish His work through His Church.

The Bible is rich with directives for making lay ministries effective. It gives guidance for healthy relationships between leaders and congregants, more specifically between pastors and parishioners. It is important to read and reread the playbook and to follow its instructions.

Scripture helps lay leaders find ways to reenergize discouraged pastors. The Bible offers God's wisdom, correction and perspective to help us shake off lethargy. In the process, every congregation is enriched by pastors and lay leaders who live according to biblical teaching.

GOD WANTS LAY LEADERS DEVELOPED BY PASTORS

It was [Christ] who gave some to be apostles, some to be prophets, some to be evangelists, and some to be pastors and teachers, to prepare God's people for works of service, so that the body of Christ may be built up until we all reach unity in the faith and in the knowledge of the Son of God and become mature, attaining to the whole measure of the fullness of Christ (Eph. 4:11-13).

In a world where confidence in the Church appears to be at an all-time low, good pastors are needed more than ever. Pastors are needed to lead people to Christ and to help every believer become more Christlike. Ephesians 4:11-13 has become a favorite preaching passage for making the point that one of a pastor's main responsibilities is "to prepare God's people for works of service."

But there is much more in these verses because of their context. In this passage, the apostle Paul lists nine significant reasons why pastors are needed:

1. To build up the Body of Christ
2. To assist believers in achieving unity in the faith
3. To expand our knowledge of the Son of God
4. To facilitate our maturity
5. To aid us in attaining the whole measure of the fullness of Christ
6. To encourage our growth so we will not be deceived by counterfeit teachings
7. To call us to speak the truth in love
8. To help us grow up in Christ
9. To stimulate Christian love so the Body of Christ will be built up as each part does its work

As you review Paul's reasons as to why pastors are needed, notice who addresses these nine necessities—pastors. Eugene H. Peterson, long-time pastor and more recently a trainer of pastors, insightfully paraphrases the passage.

[Christ] handed out gifts of apostle, prophet, evangelist, and pastor-teacher to train Christians in skilled servant work, working within Christ's body, the church, until we're all moving rhythmically and easily with each other, efficient and graceful in response to God's Son, fully mature adults, fully developed within and without, fully alive like Christ.

No prolonged infancies among us, please. . . . His [Christ's] very breath and blood flow through us, nourishing us so that we will grow up healthy in God, robust in love (Eph. 4:11-13, *THE MESSAGE*).

CHERISH PASTORS IN LOVE

In 1 Thessalonians 5:12-13, Paul instructs his readers,

> We ask you, brothers, to respect those who work hard among you, who are over you in the Lord and who admonish you. Hold them in the highest regard in love because of their work. Live in peace with each other.

In explaining the meaning of this passage, New Testament scholar William Barclay wrote,

> The reason for the respect is the work the minister is doing. It is not a question of personal prestige; it is the task which makes a man great, and it is the service that he is doing that is his badge of honor.[1]

Although we do not know what organizational pattern existed between clergy and laypeople in Thessalonica, Paul, using strong language, calls upon (or exhorts) the Church to cherish its spiritual leaders. He gives three reasons.

1. Cherish Them for Their Work's Sake

First Thessalonians 5:12 instructs Christians to "respect those who work hard among you." Authentic ministry is hard work, not for weaklings or slackers. Unlike the physical toil of a ditch digger or carpet layer, this work requires listening to people tell of their hurts, studying the Word, warning people about the consequences of sin and always being available to meet the needs of other people.

A pastor also needs to show incredible self-discipline. He is compelled to keep his lips zipped, smile and display a positive attitude when a lay leader who runs into him at 9 P.M. at the local pharmacy suggests that he lives an easy life. He has to do this even if he started that day before breakfast with a visit to the hospital where he sat with the family of a member who was having cancer surgery. He must do it even after he has spent three hours preparing his sermon, chaired a finance subcommittee meeting at lunch, made six hospital calls in the afternoon and led a Bible study in the evening. He is obliged to do it even if the reason for his visit to the pharmacy is to pick up a prescription for a homebound parishioner or for a sick member of his own family.

2. Cherish Them for Their Leadership in the Lord

Pastors can lead like a CEO in a Fortune 500 company if they wish. But a minister's unique task is to keep the people in his or her church connected to Christ in every dimension of life. That takes understanding and empowerment from God. It takes spiritual authority that calls people to holy living. This demands a kind of leadership that is different from that of any other occupation and is best lived out as the minister invites people "to come follow me as I follow Christ."

3. Cherish Them When They Admonish You

"Admonish" means "to instruct *and* warn." Admonishing happens through preaching and teaching, which are two of the most important roles of a pastor. Just as a child is taught not to cross a busy street, a pastor's admonition is not a mere safety lecture but a warning, "Keep out of the street! A car is coming!" In the church, the one who admonishes does not give take-it-or-leave-it advice. He communicates the Word of God that must be followed because it really matters. First Thessalonians 5:12, *THE MESSAGE,* describes people who have been "admonished" as those "who have been given the responsibility of urging and guiding you along in your obedience."

After showing why spiritual leaders are so significant to the church and the individual believer, Paul urges congregations to overwhelm them with appreciation and love!

FOLLOWERS FOLLOW *AND* LEAD

During the season of magnificent grapes, the Lord instructed Moses to send spies to check out Canaan, a land God promised to give the Israelites (see Num. 13:2). The questions the spies asked before the trip sound like those asked in many contemporary church decision-making meetings: Are the people strong or weak, few or many? Is the soil fertile or barren? Is there much fruit? Do they have many trees?

Forty days after the spies were sent out, they returned with so many clusters of grapes that it took two men to carry them. They also brought back beautiful pomegranates and juicy figs and told Moses, "[The land] certainly does flow with milk and honey, and this is its fruit" (Num. 13:27, *NASB*). The food was plentiful, but there was a problem. Enemies—the descendants of Anak and others—lived on the land and in the hills. One group of spies contended that Moses and his followers could nonetheless take possession. But others concluded that the enemy was too strong (see Num. 13:28–33).

The masses began grumbling against Moses. They said they wished they had died in Egypt or out in the desert. They groused, "Let's choose a new leader who will take us back to Egypt" (see Num. 14:4). Look at their foolish thinking and their silly words: "Wouldn't it be nice to choose a leader who would help us leave the Promised Land, take us back across the desert, have us cross the Red Sea in the opposite direction, and ask Pharaoh to enslave us again? We want a leader who will lead us in a backward retreat" (see Num. 14:3).

When we consider this passage's lessons for contemporary congregations, we realize we are blessed. Like many churches, the people of Israel did not realize how blessed they were. Although their situation was not perfect, they were closer to the Promised Land than they had ever been. But because they had not reached their destination, they were ready to give up just as they stood on the edge of receiving the full benefit of God's promise.

> *We need to avoid absurd notions about the good old days and be realistic about current possibilities.*

Thank God for progress. We need to avoid absurd notions about the good old days and be realistic about current possibilities. No thinking person wants more slavery, bondage, deserts, Red Seas and pharaohs. There was nothing to go back to in Egypt. The Kingdom's direction is always forward. God's order is "Forward, march."

Resist the Grasshopper Complex

Listen to the discouraging talk of the 10 spies: "We look like grasshoppers to the people of Canaan and to ourselves" (see Num. 13:33). This group inferiority complex is rooted in a contagious spiritual forgetfulness of what God has already done for us. It is a real-life example of a group who did not recognize what God wanted to do through them in the present and future. The grasshopper complex continues to waft through and stymie hundreds of contemporary churches.

However, God will enable every church to be more than it thinks it can be. Every church leader can do more than he or she has ever imagined. We have been providentially placed at this point in history to do the redemptive work of Jesus.

We have a message and a quality way of life to share with everyone. There is no reason to be ashamed of what God planted, watered and is bringing to fruition.

Stop Grumbling

When we reread the account from Numbers, we find that the leaders faced serious problems: "The whole assembly talked about stoning them" (14:10). Contemporary churches do the same thing but use different weapons. When group members resist the will of God, they usually grumble about leaders. They feel the need to blame someone else. That is exactly what the people of Israel did. They wanted a new leader for the wrong reasons—they wanted to go back into bondage! They wanted to give up and miss God's plan for them.

Think a long time before you murmur against your spiritual leader. Refuse to convey a negative spirit. Can you see the difference in Caleb's positive attitude? He said, "We should go up and take possession of the land, for we can certainly do it" (Num. 13:30). He sounds like a visionary pastor. But then the negativity started: "They spread . . . a bad report about the land they had explored" (v. 32).

Direct descendants of these doubters are still with us. They murmur in the vestibule, in the parking lot and over cell phones. Without realizing it, negative talkers spread a contagious spirit that keeps churches wandering in the desert for years.

Note the results for the Israelites. The consequences went beyond anything they could have imagined. For 40 more years, they and their children wandered around the desert, with sand blowing in their hair, eyes and teeth. They grumbled about how dangerous it was to go into the Promised Land without giving a thought to how risky it was to stay outside of it.

Avoid Poisonous Humor

The Israelites used sarcasm to reinforce their negative views. They joked, "Was it because there were no graves in Egypt that you brought us to the desert to die?" (see Exod. 14:11). Like us, they found it easy to undermine the direction of God by using sick humor. It happens often in church decision-making groups.

In response, God was not amused when He asked Moses, "How long will these people treat me with contempt? How long will they refuse to believe in me, in spite of all the miraculous signs I have performed among them?" (Num. 14:11). When tempted to use derision in decision-making groups, lay leaders must examine themselves to see if their so-called humor is diverting the group's attention from what God wants the church to be and do.

Every decision requires energy and produces consequences. Often delayed action or retreat requires as much energy as it does to go full speed ahead. This was true for the children of Israel because most of their investment of energy took place long before the events of Numbers 13 and 14. This is a wonderful lesson for today's church.

Do Not Delay

Obviously, few Israelites considered the possibility that they would wander around for 40 more years before entering the Promised Land. Because of the delay, nearly two generations of people died before Israel entered the Promised Land. Although there are risks in moving ahead, there are also consequences for delay. Be warned—nonaction, delays and efforts to hinder progress carry high price tags.

Decisions must be viewed in light of how God sees them. In discussing not going into the Promised Land, the complainers said almost nothing about how the power of God could see them through. Joshua and Caleb told the whole assembly,

> The land we passed through and explored is exceedingly good. If the LORD is pleased with us, he will lead us into that land, a land flowing with milk and honey, and will give it to us. Only do not rebel against the LORD. And do not be afraid of the people of the land, because we will swallow them up. Their protection is gone, but the LORD is with us (Num. 14:7-9).

Regrettably, the crowd paid no attention to these words. They made no effort to view their situation from God's perspective. In fact, they wanted to kill the messengers.

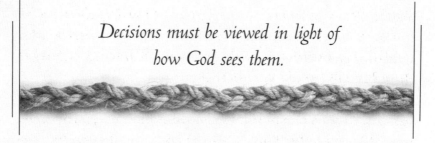

Decisions must be viewed in light of how God sees them.

God has always been faithful to His people, and He still is. He has brought us through dangers we did not see. How can lay leaders turn their backs on the power and promises of God? He promises us that the gates of hell will not prevail against the Church. The battle is His. Since we have His empowerment, we have no excuse for standing around the perimeters, wondering whether He wants us to move forward.

God is greater than any obstacle. The world needs the Church now more than ever before. This means we must see our churches as powerful instruments of holy righteousness in the hands of God. He will enable us to do everything He wants done.

Be a Loyal Follower

Human leaders need loyal followers. Business management gurus claim that no one can be a leader who is not a follower. In the church we make too many distinctions between leading and following. Realistically, in most of us, the two occur simultaneously. For example, I (H. B.) am a man, husband, father, grandfather, pastor, preacher, teacher and writer. I cannot completely sort out the distinctions, because I am all of these at the same time.

Leadership is like that, too. I am a leader and follower, a teacher and learner. Often a leader does well to follow those whom he leads. Sometimes the followers know where the pleasant paths, quiet waters and land mines are located. In this account from Numbers, most Israelites chose to fantasize about a leader who required no risks. Apparently a make-believe leader was more attractive to them than a flesh-and-blood person who wanted to move ahead to the Promised Land and reminded them that God would be with them.

No leader can lead without faithful followers who commit to see that the church fulfills Christ's mission. Your pastor needs to hear you say, "We know God has given you dreams for this church. We want you to take us into the Promised Land." God, Moses, Joshua and Caleb could not take their people where they did not want to go. Neither can your pastor.

Hold On to the Vision

Visions are easily clouded, or even destroyed. The children of Israel could not see up close what they envisioned from afar. Apparently something happened on the way that corroded their dreams. Maybe the long journey dulled their vision. Maybe repetitive routines caused the loss. Maybe a boring, repetitive regimen usurped their passion for the ways of God. Maybe they convinced each other to believe the dream would never come true.

Like a fire, a vision of Christ's mission has to be periodically stirred and refueled. The Israelites' choice clearly teaches us that we are defeated when we doubt. They demonstrate that if we say we cannot, we will not. The vision, however, becomes bigger than life when we realize God works miracles through us. A clear vision, properly communicated, produces an inner energy that is invincible.

Use Your Influence

Leaders must use their influence. Some of the Israelites who created the greatest havoc for Moses are not even named in Numbers. But, with their negative talk and dream-shattering antics, they kept the group hostage to their doubts and fears. The same sad scenario happens in churches today. Often, the naysayers have been around for years. Sometimes they are responsible for a no vote even though they are not elected to a church office.

If you are a lay leader, you have influence. Use it. This may involve taking some risks, but staying in the desert and longing for Egypt has shortcomings, too. Some contemporary churches may be only a few feet away from their Promised Lands, so why do they choose to die in their deserts?

Be Different

You do not have to follow the lead of the Israelites. You and your church can be different. To become your favorite church, let lay leaders and other church members commit to move forward in faith. Counteract and correct every negative rumor. Speak positively about your pastor's vision. Crowd the doubters with faith talk and positive perspectives. Always show people who are not in the decision-making process how God is helping your congregation fulfill its mission.

In Search of Spiritually Authentic Lay Leaders

Several years ago Fletcher Spruce published a list of spiritual qualities that laypeople should possess. He called this soul-searching list, which we have included below, *Fine Lines for Laymen*; it is based on 1 Timothy 3.

Bite your tongue (v. 8).

Some people talk so much it appears they are double-tongued. John Wesley suggested that it is impossible to hold a conversation more than 30 minutes without saying something that shouldn't be said. Think about that.

Watch your priorities (v. 8).

"Not pursuing dishonest gain" means that work, saving and accumulation are not the highest priority. Are you being kicked to death by the golden calf? The test of prosperity may be more difficult than the test of poverty.

Keep free from addictions (v. 8).

This verse warns about wine, but other addictions kill a layperson's service too, like tobacco, drugs, prescription medicine, food and gossip.

Cultivate radiant religion (v. 9).

The Living Bible translates the passage, "earnest, whole-hearted followers of Christ who is the hidden Source of their faith." The religion lay leaders need is not the kind of faith that leaves you cold, with an anemic witness and a cloudy conscience. Calvary's fountain can wash away frustrations, guilt complexes and the twisting tensions of life and bring you the beauty of Christlikeness. Keep the awe, the wonder, the breathless adoration of the Savior in your heart.

Take faith home with you (v. 12).
Good religion works at home as well as in church. A well-managed household is required for a lay leader in the church.

Be faithful in all things (v. 11).
That's the mark of righteous people. They are so dependable that they will come to church in stormy weather, stand by the pastor even when he makes a mistake, pay their tithe as sure as they make their mortgage payments and take their witnessing into the marketplace. Scripture is right: they "gain a good standing for themselves and also great confidence in the faith which is in Christ Jesus" (v. 13).[2]

GIVE PASTORS DOUBLE HONOR

Here in these early years of a new century, when pastors are at such risk, lay leaders have an excellent opportunity to rethink their ideas about their relationships with their pastors. This is a good time to significantly increase affirmation for every minister of the gospel. Consider the apostle Paul's idea. He wrote, "Elders who direct the affairs of the church well are worthy of *double honor*, especially those whose work is preaching and teaching" (1 Tim. 5:17, emphasis added).

The passage is clear. According to Paul, double honor goes to those who shape and serve the church with their preaching and teaching. Although biblical scholars may disagree about the precise definition of "double honor," it must mean more than many churches currently give their pastors. The command can infer monetary gifts, respect or affection—most pastors can use more of all three.

> *A pastor's ability to be effective is directly affected by how much respect or disdain he or she gets from lay leaders.*

Barclay summarizes the concept this way: "The minister whom the church really honored was to be the minister who worked to edify and build up the church by his preaching of truth to people, and his educating of the young and the new converts in the Christian way."[3] A pastor's ability to be effective is directly affected by how much respect or disdain he or she gets from lay leaders (see 1 Tim. 5:17-22,24-25). Author Paul Barackman shines a bright light of reality on the honor issue:

It is a fact that except for those in high places, servants of the church have never been provided for with much generosity. The church of Jesus Christ may well be proud, and humbled as well, that through the years so many dedicated men and women have borne privation of this world's goods that they might minister to the church. Ability to preach and teach the gospel is a gift not found every day. It deserves to be valued more highly than it is.[4]

Try giving your pastor double honor, but be careful because he may be shocked. Give your pastor more encouragement, more support, more friendship and more money because it is the right thing to do. Speak well of your pastor and pray for him. A congregation that honors its pastor has a good start toward becoming an authentic New Testament church.

Doubling and tripling love and honor for your pastor can produce several amazing surprises. A church that cherishes its leader often prospers in many tangible ways.

- Fulfilled pastors work harder because they are motivated by love.
- Soon a church will reflect the new perspective of the pastor.
- Lay leaders have the joy of seeing the church prosper as an authentic fellowship of believers.
- God will bless a church that does everything possible to keep its pastor spiritually, physically and emotionally healthy.

The time has come for every congregation to reevaluate and reenergize its care and affection for the pastor God has given them. It is time to strengthen ministers everywhere. Come alongside the man or woman of God who leads your church. Pray with him. Sacrifice with her. Stand beside him on good days and on bad ones. Cherish your pastor for work's sake. Pray for his spiritual prosperity. Thank God every time you think about her. In this confusing epoch of human history, God wants His Church to be strong and valiant; that cannot happen without spiritually vibrant shepherds.

The Head and Owner of the Church wants every pastor loved into greatness, encouraged into nobility and inspired into making God's will a delightful reality. When pastors succeed spiritually and feel loved by the members of their congregations, they will lead the spiritual revolution the world needs.

RENEWAL STRATEGIES FOR LAY LEADERS: FOLLOW WHAT THE BIBLE SAYS

1. Give your pastor double honor for his or her work's sake.
2. Cherish your pastor's preaching.
3. Realize your church is blessed by your pastor's efforts.
4. Resist the grasshopper mentality.
5. Stop grumbling, and get to work.
6. Be faithful in every Christian service responsibility.
7. Avoid destructive humor.
8. Remember that your pastor's dreams may be fragile.
9. Challenge influencers to use their influence for good.
10. Continuously scrutinize your own priorities.

Notes
1. William Barclay, *The Daily Study Bible: The Letters to the Philippians, Colossians and Thessalonians* (Philadelphia: Westminster Press, 1957), p. 239.
2. Fletcher Spruce, *Fine Lines for Laymen* (Kansas City, MO: Beacon/Standard, n.d.), n.p.
3. William Barclay, *The Daily Study Bible: The Letters to Timothy, Titus and Philemon* (Edinburgh, Scotland: St. Andrews Press, 1956), p. 134.
4. Paul Barackman, *Proclaiming the New Testament: The Epistles to Timothy and Titus Commentary* (Grand Rapids, MI: Baker Books, 1964), p. 65.

Do You want my hands, Lord, to spend the day helping

the sick and the poor who need them?

Lord, today I give You my hands.

Do You want my feet, Lord, to spend the day visiting

those who need a friend?

Lord, today I give You my feet.

Do You want my voice, Lord, to spend the day speaking

to all who need Your words of love?

Lord, today I give You my voice.

Do You want my heart, Lord, to spend the day loving

everyone without exception?

Lord, today I give You my heart.

MOTHER TERESA, *LIFE IN THE SPIRIT*

CHAPTER 6

OVERCOMING MYTHS ABOUT LEADERSHIP

HOW TO CREATE STRONG BONDS BETWEEN PASTORS AND LAY LEADERS

Lord of the Church, empower us to
  see past myths that blind us,
  overlook differences that divide us,
  suspect bad ideas that sandpaper us,
  intercede for the pastor who leads us,
  seek the righteousness You promised us,
  so that we may lovingly win those who have lost
    their way.
Amen.

"I feel shackled by silly notions and outdated traditions," said a frustrated Christopher McWilliams, who had recently joined the pastoral staff at Community Church. "No one seems willing to change or even discuss it."

To encourage a thoughtful dialogue, McWilliams's mentor, Pastor Phillip Kelly, acted as if he did not understand. McWilliams explained, "If I were a physician, I could discuss symptoms with my patients. Then we would make a diagnosis, find a remedy and get them back on the road to health. But I'm supposed to be the physician of my parishioners' souls, and I can't even mention some issues without offending someone. It seems church members and even lay leaders would rather keep pain in their souls or debilitating illness in their church than seek a solution. It's frustrating."

Layer upon layer of old ways of thinking, outdated notions and impractical practices keep pastors and parishioners from developing a common dream for their future together. If they could communicate openly, many of these issues would evaporate—or at least lose their sting.

The person whom we have called Pastor Kelly was right, and many pastors around the country have echoed these sentiments. That is what this chapter is about.

MYTH #1—PROBLEMS GET SMALLER WITH SILENCE

How many times have you heard someone say "I don't want to talk about it"? When you deny problems, you are closing your eyes to symptoms of a disease. Left alone long enough, the disease can be lethal. Think of what untreated diseases cause: chronic discomfort, acute pain, loss of motor or mental skills, or death.

The same is true with destructive symptoms of problems in a church. Saying "I don't see a problem" or "I don't want to talk about it" never helps.

For example, consider the troubles a financial shortfall causes. The problem, when ignored, creates persistent pain and can cripple or result in the elimination of some areas of ministry. When funds are cut, a less obvious but harmful problem follows, because people who serve in those ministries lose interest or settle for a minimal effort. Continuous underfunding hurts the cause, turns neglected maintenance into major repairs and dries up giving for missions. It is better to be forthright. Tell the church members about the problem and ask for their support through increased giving.

Many people who advocate delays or no discussion do not realize that ignored problems never go away; instead, they usually get bigger. Nonaction is usually a by-product of decision-making group members who possess little courage, do not know a method for correcting the difficulty or lack the will to act. In these situations, the church suffers and the pastor lives with unending frustration over dreams of what might have been.

Action, remedy and surgery are ways an effective doctor deals with a physical ailment. He knows the difference between a scratch on the thumb and a tumor on the brain. A scratch heals naturally, but a tumor demands immediate attention. In either case, a decision must be made about how to deal with the problem. In a church, most problems are not life threatening but many are life sapping. Whether you are a doctor examining a patient or a leader examining congregational life, when making a corrective decision you need to be forthright.

Sometimes the best way to deal with a problem is to wait for the right moment. If your reason for delaying action is well founded, then it is not denial. Quaker Emmet Fox offers a creative way to wait before acting: "To leave a thing in God's hands does not mean simply to hand it over to God, and then forget all about it . . . it means that every time the subject comes to mind you affirm that God is solving the problem in His own good way, and that all will be well."[1]

To have trust in God is different from closing your heart to a matter.

MYTH #2—YOUR OPINION IS THE TRUTH

Pastors and lay leaders often think and sometimes say "I'm usually right." Stating an opinion such as this by using forceful words or displaying a stubborn spirit muddies the decision-making process. It makes it difficult for you to use your reverse gear when you find that you have been wrong. It also makes it difficult for people who usually side with you to suggest alternatives. Thus, leaders with the most rigid opinions often feel alone or ignored, yet they do not understand why. The problem is that others do not know how to respond, so they do not say anything.

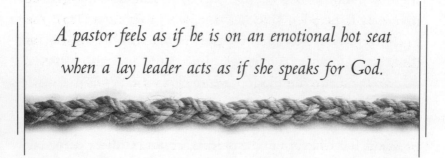

A pastor feels as if he is on an emotional hot seat when a lay leader acts as if she speaks for God.

When you state a subjective viewpoint, it is only an opinion and you should label it as such. Do not lose sight of the fact that God's truth is bigger than any of us can imagine. He has thousands of ways to solve problems. Thus, there is room for many opinions and perspectives as we seek the Father's guidance.

This dilemma can cause huge misunderstandings in decision-making groups, particularly when a lay person speaks *ex cathedra*. A pastor feels as if he is on an emotional hot seat when a lay leader acts as if she speaks for God. It is a difficult position. If the minister questions the opinion, he appears to be questioning God. Conversely, if he agrees with the statement on its merit, others think they are being denied their right to address the issue—and in a way, they are.

Without realizing it, those who believe their opinions are always, or usually, right often try to control decisions by saying "God told me" or "I'm surprised that you have followed Christ so long and still think that way!" or "It's a proven fact that . . . ." Fair-minded listeners always enjoy a bit of mischievous glee when another member of the group replies "Oh, really?" or "What makes you believe that?"

If you do Kingdom work in groups, you might want to consider using this story to help put the presuppositions and opinions of group members in proper perspective. A witness in a courtroom was about to be sworn in with the traditional oath, "Do you swear to tell the truth, the whole truth and nothing but the truth, so help you God?" The man replied, "Sir, if I told the truth, the whole truth and nothing but the truth, I would be God."[2]

Strengthen your influence and acceptance as a leader by making a clear distinction in your thinking and speaking between opinion and fact. The Canadian poet Sir William Drummond, who lived near the turn of the twentieth century, offers incredible insight for the strong opinions we often hear in committee meetings. He said, "He who will not reason is a bigot; he who cannot reason is a fool; and he who does not reason is a slave."[3]

Let's be candid. Most of us have biased conclusions about some issues. What we do not like or understand we assume is unworkable or useless. This reality shows up in our reactions to music worship styles, service schedules, color choices in remodeling projects and how the church treats visitors.

Be careful that you do not put your pastor in an administrative box so that he feels as if he is a hostage to your viewpoints. Most pastors love working with people who have the ability to think and the courtesy to allow others to have their own opinions.

In 1690, the philosopher John Locke correctly observed, "New opinions are always suspect, and usually opposed, without any other reason but because they are not already common."[4] Share your ideas quietly and then allow the sun of the Spirit and the rain of common sense to nourish them.

Myth #3—Someone Must Be Blamed

Often, after a problem is discovered, the first words said are "Who caused it?" Blaming and shaming often place millstones around a congregation's heart. Blame sometimes mesmerizes a church and prevents it from becoming what God intended it to be.

The most important facets in refusing to play the blame game is for individuals to accept responsibility for their conduct, to own what is rightfully theirs and then show the same mercy to others that they hope others will show them.

Today's blame can cause far-reaching consequences that a church finds difficult to overcome. Many decades ago, a vocal minority in a church near where we live blamed a staff member for making a $5,000 mistake. They called the incident stealing and insisted on taking it to civil court. The judge threw the matter out of court, calling it a mischief suit. That judgment should have ended the matter, but it did not. Blaming became the order of the day, mostly because of the embarrassment the civil suit caused in the community. Soon a vocal minority pulled out to plant a new church. Those who stayed with the original church, as might be expected, were forced to prune existing ministries because of decreased income. The accused staff member was branded for life. As a result, he lived under a cloud of unwarranted suspicion. And though most people have forgotten the court case, petty problems still fester that can be traced to the blaming and shaming from more than four decades ago. To this day, the church started by dissenters has a contentious congregational personality that causes an unhealthy environment for members and anyone who visits. Over the years, many who did the most finger pointing have moved on because even they did not like the kind of church they had helped create.

Refusing to blame promotes peace and allows room for errors that are a natural by-product of risk-taking. Refusing to blame gives others the benefit of the doubt and makes forgiveness possible. It also forces decision-making group members to look for solutions rather than culprits.

A serendipity for the soul often flows to those who refuse to blame. They build up emotional and spiritual capital, so others are not so apt to blame them when they do something silly or ridiculous. We love the accepting attitude of the old father in the biblical story of the prodigal son. He had no time to blame because he celebrated what mattered so much more to him—his son was home.

MYTH #4—CONFLICT MUST BE AVOIDED AT ANY COST

Some people avoid conflict and insist at keeping peace at any price. Since the church is the only organization committed to the loving acceptance of everyone, internal conflict should not surprise us. Even the disciples argued about greatness in the presence of Jesus (see Mark 9:34).

The church that seeks to avoid conflict at any cost should not expect to get much done for the Kingdom. All progress requires change for someone. Change often creates resistance and resistance means conflict. The only way to completely avoid conflict is for everyone to live and work alone—an impossibility because the church, by its essence, requires people to serve together.

Leaders often worry needlessly about possible conflict. Many of the problems that might be expected to hurt the church, resulting from disagreements, never happen. Calvin Coolidge's advice applies: "Never go out to meet trouble. If you will just sit still, in nine out of ten cases someone will intercept it before it reaches you."[5]

In any group organized around democratic principles there will be differences. For example, a five-person committee in one church consisted of a policeman, an insurance-agency owner, a factory worker, a mechanic and a truck driver. Their diversity created a richness within the group, but they still needed to develop patience as they learned to work with each other.

Conflict in the church, then, must be viewed as an inescapable fact of life. The objective is to manage conflict so it is creative and useful—not destructive. In the church, this means allowing, or even expecting and encouraging, people to share their best thoughts on a subject. There should always be room for people to stand up for what they believe, providing it is done in humility and with respect for others.

Pastors are often disheartened when people do not speak their minds in a meeting. He is frustrated by those who must have their own way at any cost. And he is grievously disappointed by those who speak freely outside formal meetings but are silent inside meetings. You can aid the progress of your church by leading an effort to accept the fact that conflict is real and that it can be useful.

Myth #5—Nitpickers and Perfectionists Should Not Be Offended

Two self-appointed critics who called themselves informants made an appointment to meet a minister on a Monday morning. After normal pleasantries, they announced their intention to share their not-so-inspiring findings. Here's the essence of their conversation: "Now, pastor, we want you to know we appreciate you, but we thought you would like to know what people are saying—things you will probably want to improve. Mrs. Recreational Talker says that you are spending too much time with new people. Mrs. I. M. Whiner says that in your pastoral prayer you no longer thank God for new babies. Mr. Fussy says the shut-ins are complaining because you do not visit them often enough. Miss Particular says you don't mingle with people after the worship service. And we wonder, pastor, if our church is friendly enough." Although these two well-intentioned informants did not mean to kill the pastor, they nearly nibbled him to death.

Most pastors want to be informed about issues that matter, but every church has nitpickers who always have complaints. A chief source of pain for a pastor is the regret she feels when someone in a congregation expects more than she is able to give. And this anguish especially cuts to the heart when a pastor is involved in ministries that cannot be discussed, such as providing pastoral care to a couple determined to divorce, offering support to a family whose daughter is pregnant out of wedlock, ministering to a family whose son is dying of AIDS which he contracted while attending a Christian college or spending time with the finance committee chairman to figure out how to cope with a deficit caused when five giving families moved out of the area.

Lay leaders can protect pastors from nitpickers by helping their spiritual leaders keep ministry in perspective and by gently helping nitpickers see the big picture. Sometimes nitpickers need to be confronted with one word—STOP!

Here are some solid principles for pastors and lay leaders:

Evaluate
Since not all criticism is accurate, it must be sorted out.

Ignore
Some criticism comes from recreational talkers who mean no harm and expect no changes.

Seek Discernment
In personal spiritual development, pastors and lay leaders should

seek guidance to distinguish what is important from what is trivial.

Protect

Lay leaders should protect the pastor from unreasonable criticism. This can be accomplished by having an active pastoral-relations committee that serves as a two-way screening group to evaluate any complaints about the pastor and to discuss concerns raised by the pastor.

Volunteer

Legitimate concerns can be delegated to lay leaders. Go ahead, step forward.

Laugh

While everyone deserves a fair hearing, sometimes pastors and lay leaders have to learn to laugh at some ridiculous demands.

Keep this reality in mind—your minister is not a superpastor. The most anyone should expect is that the pastor will do his reasonable best—and that should be good enough. It certainly is good enough from God's perspective.

MYTH #6—WHAT HAS BEEN MUST ALWAYS BE

How many times has a change not been made in your church because someone said "We've always done it that way"? In almost every generation, reform or revival springs up as a reaction against empty forms and lifeless traditions. These movements start out with the purpose of taking the essence of the Christian faith to the cutting edge of its time. Yet after a few years, the new group finds itself defending and propagating its traditions, often out-traditionalizing earlier generations.

The Christian faith has some traditions we never want to lose, such as singing hymns, preaching the Word, receiving the sacraments and fellowshiping. But other traditions are not sacred at all—for example, when we have the Christmas program, where fellowship activities are held, where the pastor lives, who plays the organ, when services are held, what our style of worship is, who counts the offerings and what the pastor's spouse does in ministry.

One country church has a long-established tradition that the oldest male member serves as head usher. What a sad show-and-tell of how debilitating tradition can be when you see an arthritic old man trying to fulfill his duty.

More churches are dying for change than are dying because of change.

The winds of rapid transition are blowing everywhere. Our forefathers often had generations to adjust, but today we have to be like superman going into the telephone booth—we sometimes have only a few weeks or months to change. The winds are blowing at top speeds, and the storm is not likely to slow down anytime soon. There is no need to fear: When God designed the Church, He made it strong enough to face storms, perform rescue efforts and rebuild what the enemy would tear down. Traditions are good when they are celebrated but they are deadly when worshiped.

Every pastor needs to be able to choose how to do ministry. As church leaders, take responsibility for being a go-between for an innovative pastor and the defenders of traditions. Try to explain prevailing traditions to a new pastor and encourage her to make changes meaningfully and with full explanations. At the same time, when the pastor suggests changes, champion the cause, promote the possibilities, run interference with nitpickers and become her advocate to appropriate decision-making groups.

More churches are dying for change than are dying because of change. Although business writer John Cowan probably did not have the Church in mind, his advice is useful: "Usually all the distracting noises in an organization in flux turn out to be just noises. Focus on what you are trying to do. Do it."[6]

Try to keep a long-term view. Remember that today's revolutionary ideas will likely be tomorrow's staid traditions. One church I (Neil) served, after much debate, instituted what they considered to be a revolutionary idea: having a living Lord's supper at Easter. The saints resisted with a thousand questions about precedent, cost, church dramatics and grown men walking barefoot in church. That church now advertises this service as a 30-year tradition and members look forward to the event— it's something they would not want to miss. In my heart, I wonder if the ritual has lost its meaning, but I pity any pastor who tries to change it. Traditions are like that.

MYTH #7—MY EXCUSES ARE VALID

You have probably heard most of the excuses: "I didn't know what was expected." "I didn't have enough time." "My committee let me down." "It took more time than I thought." "I was afraid to take too much authority." "I was shocked at the price, so I thought you might want to reconsider." Perhaps you have even used these excuses yourself. Excuses are a way we let ourselves off for making service to Christ in the church a low priority.

Rationalizations about our time commitments melt like ice in the summer sun when we consider this reality check by Vance Havner: "While we are puttering, life gets away. . . . We are so busy with the here and now that we forget the eternal. If you are too busy to find time for God, you are too busy. You have received a charge to keep, and if your busyness keeps you from being about your Father's business, you are a poor business-man."[7]

Ouch!

The exceedingly slow pace of deciding, acting and achieving frustrates pastors, especially when they see how quickly we get things done in our personal lives and in our jobs. We cannot rationalize our behavior by saying "I'm only a volunteer." After all, who was it that volunteered to serve?

MYTH #8—MY EXPERIENCE WORKS IN EVERY SITUATION

People who have been in the church a long time will often try to help and say "This is the way it worked in our other church." No church is like it once was or like the one of our childhood. Like a sleepy creek in the country that looks as it did in bygone years, the church constantly changes in subtle, almost imperceptible ways. But it changes continuously.

That reality is hard to accept. When we hear the word "church," most of us do not think about the Bible's definition, what the ancient creeds declare or what theology explains. Instead, we usually think of the little church in the wild wood or the beautiful edifice on Main Street or the storefront chapel in an urban neighborhood. "Church"—the grand old word associated with the warm family feeling from our past—creates as many mental images as there are people to think them. Our memories are a lot like the elderly man who reminisced, "My baseball batting skills keep getting better as I grow older." Our ideas about church and its meaning in our past grow more tender and more nostalgic but less accurate with passing years. So we idealize the past and wish we could re-create a church like the one we think we remember.

Lead your church to live in the present moment in an exciting relationship with Christ.

What is gone is gone, but new ways must be found to make ministry effective now. Thus, the issue is not technique, tradition or past ritual but impact, influence and Christ-exalting relationships for today.

To help a pastor keep focused on ministry in the present, lay leaders should avoid universalizing their church experiences from the past. They must focus on today. Lead your church to live in the present moment in an exciting relationship with Christ and in satisfying associations with each other.

MYTH #9—OUR PASTOR SHOULD DO BETTER

How many pastors have heard a church member say "I wish we had a stronger leader"? A pastor we shall call Stephen Smith had faults that his church members easily recognized. But Stephen also had many strengths. He cared for his congregation and showed it. He preached well, so his sermons were always biblical, thoughtful and occasionally confrontational. Some considered him distant, but he was really shy. Some thought he was too studious, though he was really serious about understanding the meaning of Scripture and applying it to life. Some thought his marriage and children had too high a place in his priorities; he was actually committed to avoiding problems in his family that his "absentee father" caused in his childhood. In fact, Stephen's commitment to his family was a beautiful model of Christian marriage and parenting. In order to be sacrificial with his stewardship, he was frugal in his lifestyle and his family lived as simply as possible. Still, some church members struggled to understand his priorities.

Finally, after five years of service to his first church, Stephen accepted a call to serve another church in a town 50 miles away. He was too gracious to tell anyone the real reasons for leaving, but he wrote in his journal, "I am tired of criticism, so I think it's time to move to a new assignment."

Three months after Pastor Smith left, the church realized what they had lost. Some wondered aloud what they could have done to keep him from leaving. They were right to ask whether the situation could have been remedied with a bit more affirmation, a raise in salary, a new air-conditioning unit at the parsonage or a book allowance of $500 per year.

Maybe it is risky to ask why pastors leave. But it is a good question to consider. Like one laywoman said, "I once asked a pastor why he was leaving and he told me. I learned a lot about a pastor's financial problems. I will never ask a pastor that question again, because it makes me grieve over what we could have done to assist his family."

Every church decision-making group would do itself a great favor by regularly affirming the pastor's strengths. Celebrate his character, commitments and competencies. Honor his passionate sense of mission and his nurturing efforts for people. In such an atmosphere of accepting affirmation, many pastors will stretch to be as good as people think they should be.

> *Every church decision-making group would do itself a great favor by regularly affirming the pastor's strengths.*

A lay leader opened his heart to his former pastor, whom he had not seen in 20 years. "If only we had known what a treasure we had when you were our pastor, we would have done anything to keep you," he said. "More money, appreciation, understanding—more anything seems like a small price compared to the confusion we experienced for 10 years after you left."

Your pastor is a priceless treasure that God has given your church. Cherish his ministry and try to recognize his full value to the life of your church, to the destiny of your soul and to the spiritual growth of your own faith.

Myth #10—Confusing Carelessness with Faithfulness

Some church members are quick to blame leaders for problems. We have all heard it sometime: "You mean the Newmans are leaving the church? It can't be; he's been a lay leader for years. I hear the Thompsons are thinking about joining another church, too. Where are they going and why? The Newmans grew up in this church. It's like losing a member of our family. They say they are not being fed from the pulpit."

We live in a consumer-based society that makes it easy to move to another fellowship for shallow or even selfish reasons. But it is a kick in the stomach and a stab in the heart when a pastor hears, usually by way of the grapevine, that someone is leaving to attend a church where the people are "friendly," the preacher is "sensational" or the teaching is "deeper."

Many pastors leave the ministry permanently, because they cannot deal with their feelings of anguish over losing people they loved. Many suffer grief and a sense of loss. Often they cannot bring themselves to explain the real issues to those who remain. They feel rejected—almost abandoned and betrayed—by those they served in times of crisis. Many are just not able to shake the feeling that they failed; because they are called by God to serve people, the rejection and apparent failure hurt.

Here are ways lay leaders can help diffuse these situations:

1. Do not panic—God is in control.
2. Evaluate yourself and your church's ministry.
3. Correct flaws, blemishes and mistakes.
4. Make sure those who leave know they can come back.
5. Show kindness to all parties but downplay gossip and curiosity.
6. Accept the reality that not everyone will be happy in every church.
7. Cultivate a spirit of serving through the church rather than a spirit of taking from the church.
8. Recognize the fact that it is almost impossible to keep church hoppers happy.
9. Move ahead in victory.

10. Keep a close relationship with your pastor, like you would anyone who suffers grief.

REVERSING THE MYTHS

If you continued to listen to the discussion between Pastor Kelly and Pastor McWilliams started at the beginning of this chapter, the list of dilemmas would have grown. Every pastor and congregation have their own slate of myths. Since the items on the lists vary so much, how can all of the myths be understood and solved?

As a starting point of solution, we must get past what one minister said of his first three years in a particular church: "The first year, they idolized me; the second year, they tantalized me; and the third year, they scandalized me."

Work to improve communication between pastors and lay leaders. Some communication strategies can be structured and scheduled once every three months. Other conversations can be informal, such as lunch or dinner with the pastor and a small group of lay leaders.

Dialogue, affirmation and understanding are the goals. Although not every lay leader, pastor or decision-making group will be comfortable, efforts to improve communication need to be put in place. Initiate and design the process in whatever way works for your church, but do it.

The following discussion stimulators between leaders and pastors will start a flow of ideas. Ask your pastor these questions:

1. How close is the church to fulfilling its mission?
2. What expectations do you have that are not being fulfilled?
3. What can be done to make your ministry more effec-

    tive? Is it a new desk, a new computer or increased support staff?

4. What is the most affirming word or act you have ever received from a lay leader in any church?

5. What do you do in the church that a layperson could do as well? Or what could I do to help you?

6. Do your spouse and family feel cherished in our church? If yes, how? If no, why not?

7. What changes need to be made in our church to encourage you to remain for the next 15 years?

8. What core values is the church unintentionally overlooking?

9. If you had five uncommitted days with which to do anything you wanted, what would you do?

10. How would you adjust the present priorities in our church?

The laity always want sensitive, competent pastors. At the same time, ministers pray for committed, gifted laity that are deeply devoted to Christ. Since there are not enough ideal pastors or ideal laity to go around, you have a magnificent opportunity to help each other grow into what God wants you both to become. A common belief is that a great pastor makes a great church, and it is often true. But the converse is also true—committed laity shape and mold pastors into greatness.

Author Laurie Jones offers a grand reason for looking beyond all the debilitating church myths: "Jesus wants leaders to constantly look for ways to expand their vision, their influence and their contribution. There are always more possibilities than our eyes can see."[8]

All these possibilities provide an extraordinary opportunity for lay leaders and pastors to grow as Christians and to reenergize churches to fulfill the mission of Christ in our time.

RENEWAL STRATEGIES FOR LAY LEADERS: HELPS FOR UNMASKING THE MYTHS

1. Denying problems makes them multiply.
2. Insisting on your way destroys church unity.
3. Fixing blame on someone exaggerates problems.
4. Keeping peace at any price may be too expensive.
5. Pleasing nitpickers is impossible.
6. Worshiping the past seldom inspires renewal.
7. Testing your excuses against standards you use to judge others.
8. Recognizing every church is different and every generation in the same congregation is distinct.
9. Valuing your pastor's strengths. It will help you see past his or her weaknesses.
10. Defending your pastor's faithfulness, especially when it is being called carelessness.

Notes

1. Emmet Fox, *Making Your Life Worthwhile* (San Francisco: HarperSanFrancisco, 1946), p. 211.
2. Jan G. Linn, *What Ministers Wish Church Members Knew* (St. Louis, MO: Chalice Press, 1993), p. 11.
3. Sir William Drummond, quoted in Louis E. Boone, *Quotable Business* (New York: Random House, 1992), p. 211.
4. John Locke, "Concerning Human Understanding," quoted in *Concise Oxford Dictionary of Quotations* (Oxford, England: Oxford Press, 1994), n.p.
5. Calvin Coolidge, quoted in Boone, *Quotable Business*, p. 85.
6. John Cowan, *The Common Table* (New York: HarperBusiness, 1993), p. 83.
7. Vance Havner, *Day by Day with Vance Havner* (Grand Rapids, MI: Baker Book House, 1953), p. 164.
8. Laurie Jones, *Jesus CEO* (New York: Hyperion Publishers, 1994), p. 109.

We take our lead from Christ, who is the source of every-thing we do. He keeps us in step with each other. His very breath and blood flow through us, nourishing us so that we will grow up healthy in God, robust in love.

EPHESIANS 4:15-16, *THE MESSAGE*

CHAPTER 7

CREATING A HEALTHY SELF-CONCEPT

HOW TO MAKE YOUR CHURCH WHOLE

God our Father and Owner of the Church,
Make our congregation holy, healthy, whole.
Give us the mind of Christ.
Help us discern Your plan for the Church in
this setting and time.
Saturate our labors with the power of Christ.
Amen.

Pastors almost always have high hopes when they start serving a congregation. They assume the congregation is an authentic living cell of the everlasting Church of Jesus Christ. They believe the church is much more than a regional franchise of a certain brand of Christianity, where customers must be pleased and the local outlet must show a profitable bottom line. They enthusiastically assume pastoral leadership, expecting the church to be the people of God. Many believe their new assignment has the potential to become their dream church.

All too often, however, those dreams soon turn into nightmares. Then, like the pastors before them, after waiting it out for awhile, they pack up their hopes and take their dreams to another place.

The situation is sad. No one knows who to blame. In too many settings, the Church has a corroded self-image. It has tried to be so many things that it has forgotten the main thing. It has been criticized and beaten up, and it has turned in on itself with legalism, selfishness and pulse taking. The status quo has created apathy and dysfunction. Poor diet, lack of exercise and sheer boredom have taken their toll. Low-grade fevers and chronic illness have sapped the Church's energy. The Church has become a self-focused, spiritual hypochondriac.

We do not have to live with such dysfunction. Healing is available.

For years, vital and vibrant churches have been busy fulfilling their missions. How different they are from congregations that struggle to maintain their existence. In the first group, one characteristic is evident: a positive self-image and a healthy congregational self-concept, or wholesome self-esteem. Those congregations feel good about themselves, their work and their future. A church with a strong self-image holds its head high, possesses a lofty vision and values its importance in the community. And the members of such a church know that they play a vital role in the kingdom of God.

THE ANATOMY OF A LOW
SELF-CONCEPT CHURCH

For illustrative purposes, let's go back a few years in my (H. B.'s) ministry history to take an inside look at a tiny church whose members had a congregational self-concept that was significantly less than positive. In fact, I sometimes felt that I would not consider attending my own church if I were not the pastor.

My first church had problems related to its locale, appearance and reputation. Nestled behind a service station on a side street in a second-rate section of the city, the church could not expect new people to attend without some pretty good reason. As a result, few new people ever came.

Of course, nearly everyone thinks a church's location has little to do with self-concept, but it does. A poor location and a shabby appearance send a negative message to all who pass the church. But it also communicates a "we don't matter much" spirit to the faithful church members.

Every church location should convey a sense of welcome and show signs of vibrant life. The building, however old or limited, should declare "Someone loves this place."

Although the location of my first church could not be changed, the opinion of the location changed. The church became a happening place. All of a sudden, the site looked different to those who passed by. They saw people. They saw caring. They saw happy faces. The lights were on. Something important was taking place. When that happens, a church can develop a healthy self-image, even in a bad location. The opposite is also true. A church with a good location can have a bad self-image if nothing meaningful is happening there.

That little church had another problem: a poor reputation. Even the denominational leaders and members of neighboring churches looked down on that humble band.

Why? No one had gone to jail or stolen money. The problem was the people looked down on themselves. They had decided that they were a congregation of nobodies and that was the way it would always be. They asked themselves, "Who would want to come and join our group?" Their answer was "Nobody." They thought, *We are just forced by our circumstances to stay here in our negative little world until we all die out.*

What a dreadful way to live, and what a horrible testimony for the cause of Christ.

Lessons from the Amish

On a trip to Florida, I (H. B.) saw a great contingent of Amish people on the beach. They were dressed in plain dark clothing. The men wore casual clothes, and the women long skirts, dark stockings and head coverings. At first I felt sorry for them. *Why would they dress like that?* I thought. Don't they know they are the laughingstock of the whole beach?

But then I noticed something very interesting. These folks were not the least bit intimidated by the surroundings or by the fact they were different. They were not ashamed. They were laughing and energetic. They did not look to see what others were thinking about them. They were satisfied with their self-image and convinced of the worthwhile nature of their lifestyle. It was a meaningful moment for me. In fact, I found myself saying under my breath, "Good for you. Nice going. I'm proud of you."

These people were so different from the ones in the church I once served. It all has to do with how people feel about themselves. In a church, it has to do with how secure and comfortable we are with being what we are called to be and do.

Time to Go Fishing

The absence of purpose was the third problem area in my first ministry assignment. That church had forgotten why they were there. So many years had come and gone without any measurable results that they had grown content with merely existing. They reminded me of the man who got up early one morning. He took his fishing gear and headed for a mountain stream. He walked out into the cold water with all the equipment like he was a seasoned fisherman. He had a hat filled with nicely tied flies. He had his waders on. He had a net. He had a basket around his waist to hold the fish. He had it all. Then after a few casts, his line was tugged by a beautiful rainbow trout. He fought the fish awhile and then reeled it in so that he could use his net to capture his prize. As he stood looking at the fish, he murmured, "Can you beat that? I caught a fish!"

> *It does not matter what size your church is or how many pastors you have had. It is "fishing time."*

What did he expect? Didn't he go fishing? Didn't he prepare to catch a fish? Why would he be so surprised? Too many churches are like that. They never really expect to attract anyone, and if they do, they do not know what to do with the catch.

It does not matter what size your church is or how many pastors you have had. It is "fishing time." That's the purpose of the church—to fish for lost people, to cast out your net, to reach the lost. That is what Christ expects of you, and that is what He promised to empower you to accomplish. And that is where congregations find their greatest sense of health and well-being.

Importance of Following the Leader

Leadership was the fourth problem in that first church. There was no one to follow. The church had gone through so many pastors and had run off so many potential leaders that the members of the congregation were going nowhere. They were bogged down in their past. They had no one to help them get on course again. It was pitiful. No one wanted to make a decision, because they were afraid someone would decide something that might create a long-term problem, so they did nothing. This scenario is not unlike that of the wildebeest of Africa, who lives harder, not smarter.

I love watching television programs about nature. The migration of animals on the African plains always intrigues me. The wildebeest is at the top of my curiosity list. It is an ugly beast that is constantly on the move—it seems to never stop. To fight for survival, it travels hundreds of miles to find food and water.

Some churches are like wildebeests. With no leadership, they merely exist from one Sunday to another. When the new year comes, they start over again—doing the same thing the same way because no one says "Stop!" No one says "Let's evaluate the way we do things." No one thinks to ask "Could we do it better? Since nothing is happening, should we do it differently?"

Some of these churches do not even know why they resist change, but they do. With no improvement or progress, their constant wanderings continue. The mission program is like it always has been. The order of the worship remains the same. The decision-making group does things the way they always have. Doing the same thing the same way, year after year, produces the same meager results. Like a person with a chronic low-grade fever, these churches always feel fretful and worried about their health.

As I watched the huge herds of wildebeests in Africa on their migration route, I wondered if it could have been any different for them. For hundreds of years, new generations have lived the same way. They probably could not change, even if they were forced to. But in thinking about the church, if it does not change its habitual wanderings, in time, like the wildebeest, it may simply die out, wear itself out in its wanderings or be destroyed by predators.

The solution is to find a leader or to be a leader. We have all heard the well-worn but very profound saying "Lead, follow or get out of the way." If you are a member of a church that is like the one described here, then the saying applies. Lead, follow or get out of the way so that someone else can do something great for God in your congregation.

My first church overcame these four problems. Here are some lessons we learned in the process:

Location

It is not so much where a church is but what happens there, how the facilities look and how the congregation uses the buildings.

Reputation

Although reputation has to do with what others think of you, it is mostly dependent upon how your congregation feels about itself.

Purpose

It is not so much that you exist but why you exist. Why has God providentially established your church? What is your reason for being?

Leadership

It is not so much who is the leader but if you are following the leader to a desired goal. Are designated leaders leading? And are leaders being developed to take the church to the next level of growth and to ongoing health?

BIRTHMARKS OF A HEALTHY SELF-CONCEPT

I (H. B.) remember when my grandson, Taylor, was born. Family members were all standing around him, making sure he had all his toes and fingers. I noticed a very small birthmark on the inside of his left calf, but I do not think anyone else did. But I thought then, *Taylor will carry that little signature from God for the rest of his life.* At Thanksgiving, when we were sitting quietly playing a game, I noticed that he still carried God's special mark on his left leg.

Why a story about my grandson? Well, grandfathers have a way of slipping grandchildren stories into their speaking and writing. But this story also serves as a way to start a discussion of God's special birthmarks on His church. Here we are not referring to the whole Church of Jesus Christ but to your local church.

The church you love and care for is unique and special. What are some of its special birthmarks? We recommend that you compile a list of your own self-image birthmarks. What follows is a sample to get you started.

1. A Spirit of Confidence

Wherever you are—in malls, airports or on a street corner—people with certain physical traits catch your attention. A local church is like that. Every congregation is unique and distinctive. No other church is exactly like yours. The reason: No other church has the same group of people, mission, setting, history or future.

Have you ever thought about how some churches capture the attention of a community more than others? A church's confidence plays a large role in this. It may take many forms—the pastor, a mission program, a church's interest in teens or a senior citizens program. The possibilities are nearly endless, but something always stands out in the strong church. You may not recognize or like it, but the church, nevertheless, always projects a sense of confidence and determination and an awareness of mission.

We often wonder what the whole Church of Christ would be like if every group of believers was so dedicated to its work that it assumed a position of confidence that shows that its members believe "the battle is the LORD's" (1 Sam. 17:47) and that "if God is for us, who can be against us?" (Rom. 8:31). If we believed with full confidence in Christ and in what He wants us to do, we could easily defeat every enemy.

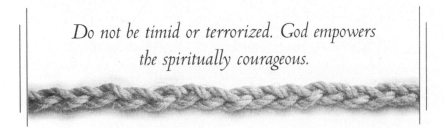

Do not be timid or terrorized. God empowers the spiritually courageous.

We want your church to have confidence like that. You are a winner on a great team owned by God Himself! Christ paid the price to make your church more than a conqueror. Hold your head high. Believe in the One who sent you. Believe in His ability to sustain you. He made you a partner with the omnipotent One. Do not be timid or terrorized. God empowers the spiritually courageous. Remember those strengthening words Paul wrote in Philippians 4:13, "I can do everything through him who gives me strength." Believe that promise—it is as dependable as the law of gravity. Trust the Lord Jesus to give you confidence in your assignment.

2. A Willingness to Risk

For church members to take a risk means they must be willing to allow the Holy Spirit to push them beyond their comfort zone to try new things. Be open to positive change, even if it is frightening. Seek to win new population groups. Take the gospel to unlikely prospects. Welcome new people.

Unless a church attempts something magnificently risky for Christ, it stands still, never invading the enemy's stronghold or succeeding in tearing down barriers. Almost every advance in Church history has required a risk on someone's part.

One of the great contemporary preachers is East Indian evangelist Samuel T. Kamaleson, who once served as a vice president at World Vision. In a letter to me (H. B.), he talked of the

Willingness to take risks has little to do with age but a lot to do with faith and trust.

risks Caleb took throughout his life. You remember, Caleb willingly took risks so he might inhabit the Promised Land. But even as an old man, he longed for an opportunity to rout the pagan enemy. About Caleb, Kamaleson wrote these inspiring words of faith:

Caleb returned from scouting Palestine to say that God would enable the children of Israel to overcome the giants who possessed the land. Years later, when Moses was parceling out the land to the tribes, Caleb, now eighty-five and still confident of God's sustaining power, claimed the territory where he had seen the giants. Caleb said, "Now give me this hill country that the LORD promised me that day. You yourself heard then that the Anakites were there and their cities were large and fortified, but, the LORD helping me, I will drive them out just as he said" (Josh. 14:12).[1]

Willingness to take risks has little to do with age but a lot to do with faith and trust. We must believe that God is just as much the God of the present and future as He is God of the past.

A congregation that believes in God will take risks like Caleb did. In the process, taking risks translates into full dependence on God. Following their victories, a congregation will have a growing positive and realistic self-image. Like Caleb, their persistence and commitment will be contagious. Over time, the whole atmosphere of the church changes for the better.

3. A Willingness to Resolve Differences

It was a moment in American history that many people missed. Remember the incident in Los Angeles when Rodney King was brutally beaten by the police? The video of that spectacle was seen the world over on television. It caused outrage among the African-American and white communities. The ramifications of the trial were monumental. But during the tempestuous proceedings, Rodney King simply asked, "Can't we all just get along?" That comment has echoed in many places in our society, and it must be heard in the church—can't we all just get along?

A church that believes in itself and has a healthy self-image finds positive ways to resolve differences because it believes every person has value. Such a church firmly believes no one has all the answers or the only answer. As a result, people listen to one another. Before issues cause misunderstandings, one person puts aside his or her wishes for the will of the whole. Power bases are dismantled and listening posts are established. Decisions are made to improve a church's ability to fulfill its mission. People genuinely care for one another. What an impression such behavior makes on outsiders, and how proud it must make our heavenly Father.

4. A Willingness to Share

A church that has a benevolent spirit takes pleasure in making life more bearable for others. We have yet to see a church, regard-less of its size, with an "others first" mind-set that did not feel good about itself.

One of the little-known, rarely mentioned characteristics of James Dobson's Focus on the Family is its willingness to respond to the needs of those who seek help. The Colorado Springs-based ministry is sometimes taken advantage of, but its determination to serve those who have needs has not been taint-ed by negative experiences. As a result of their putting others first, God has blessed Focus on the Family beyond description.

The church that finds ways to use its resources and talents for the advancement of the gospel and for the betterment of humankind will always feel good about itself. We remember the feelings that permeated the whole congregation in churches we pastored when we reached a goal that allowed us to build a church somewhere in the world, assist an inner-city ministry or provide food for the needy in our community.

5. A Willingness to Clearly Define Priorities

All of us become like what we value, because that is where we concentrate our time and energy. A church with a healthy self-image can be identified by its strong interests in the priorities of the gospel. It does not take newcomers long to see what a church values above all else.

How about your values and your church? Let's consider per-sonal priorities first. They show in what we talk about—our con-versation gives us away. They show in the pictures we display in our home and carry in our wallet. They show in the way we spend money—the Bible says our heart will be set on our trea-sure.

Another important indicator of our values are the friends whom we hold dear. It takes time and effort, sometimes sacri-fice, to be a good friend.

Our thought life is another sign of what we value in life. "As he thinketh in his heart" is the way the Bible puts it (Prov. 23:7, *KJV*).

You do not have to spend much time with an individual before you can accurately identify the things that make his existence meaningful. Use this same evaluation for your church. What kind of image does your church family have? How does the church want others to think of it?

So many churches have settled for being so much less than they could be. They have caved into pressures from the world and basically said, "We can't fight." Meanwhile, other congregations face the challenges of the enemy head-on. Although they do not win every battle, they refuse to be passive. They fight to be more than conquerors. And they succeed so many more times than their lukewarm neighbors do.

A CHECKLIST FOR CREATING A STRONG SELF-CONCEPT

There are several positive steps you can take to immediately improve your church's self-image. These corrections will blunt existing negative forces and help your congregation become a strong, effective part of the conquering Church, against which Jesus promised "the gates of hell shall not prevail" (Matt. 16:18, *KJV*).

See Your Church As Important to God and Society
Refuse to allow Satan or anyone inside or outside of your church to make you feel inferior. Look realistically at your church—remember who owns your team. Evaluate what is taking place in your church. If you find areas of ministry with less quality than our Lord deserves, improve them.

Hold your head up. Rejoice in the fact that your church is special, and believe that God has something important for your church to accomplish for Him. When you recall that Christ said He would build His Church in spite of every difficulty, your spirit will rise, and folks around you will recognize that you deeply love the Savior. Then your service for Christ through the church will be a joyful adventure. Determine to move forward at any cost. It is God's will that the church always advance.

Resist Traditional Ruts

Folk wisdom says that a rut turns into a grave if you don't keep moving. To serve this present age—which is our calling—every church must try new methods and implement innovative strategies for impacting the future. There need be no contradiction between new methods and the timeless message. The church in her finest hour throughout human history has been quick to try new methodologies while continuing to preach the changeless gospel.

Remember, every traditional practice was once an innovation someone probably said would not work. There is no spiritual merit in continuing to do things the old way just because that's the way we have always done it. Often sameness simply means we are dull in our thinking or sloppy in our planning. Over time a church that does everything the same as it always has becomes oblivious to the environment and people around it. Some new strategy or improvement is needed right now at the center of your congregation's life. Let go of your fear of change by realizing that the average person is not as opposed to innovation as many church leaders think, for the simple reason that all of us face innovation every day.

Do Not Settle for Sin and Evil

Sin and evil destroy all that is good in the human experience.

And it is so easy to get used to the dark. Do not forget that we have an enemy who hates our mission and will defeat us if he can. No church can be satisfied with resting on past blessings or yesterday's spiritual achievements. A church's self-image is always improved when it remembers it is involved in a battle for righteousness against the enemy of our souls.

Fan the Flame of Urgency

Our God-given mission is to win our neighbors and a dying world to Christ. A sense of urgency is needed. With moral standards declining all around us and church attendance shrinking, it is time to rise up and be about the mission of Christ in the world. It's time to pray and act with urgency when we see families fractured by marital conflict, when adultery is wrecking so many homes, when apathy is so prevalent and when the church has become worldly.

Intercession is needed. Diligence is required. Persistence is demanded. Devotion to the gospel is needed. A holy ruggedness is required. As Southern evangelist-statesman Vance Havner wrote years ago:

> A real Christian is a rugged, sturdy soul who is under no
> illusions about life and is grappling with things as they
> are. He is not always agreeable and sweet, for he must be
> uncompromising and firm amidst a superficial world.
> He is no lamb-like creature forever mumbling prayers
> and universally pleasant. He is a battle-scarred warrior
> who does not confuse singing an anthem with fighting
> the good fight. Being a Christian means being husky for
> heaven's sake and rugged for righteousness' sake. Better
> be out in the scrimmage and make a thousand errors
> than sit on the sidelines in blissful piety and never risk
> your idealism in the clash with reality.[2]

Renew Respect for the Appearance of Facilities

Take pride in the facilities you have. Make them as attractive as possible. A coat of paint can make a big difference. Clean windows and throw away hand-me-downs. A little hard work makes things look much better. Make your church buildings say, "Somebody loves this place." Take a realistic look at the wear and tear on your facilities, and do whatever it takes to make the house of God attractive, even beautiful.

Keep an Outreach Focus

If you were a new person seeking a church home or an unbeliever seeking Christ, would it be easy to find a happy entrance to the fellowship of your church? Try looking at all you do through the eyes of persons attending for the first time.

Too many churches lock the world out by saying unintentionally, "We are satisfied with who we are and what we have." We must be like Christ. We must open our hearts to anyone who needs love and acceptance. Please don't let your church be comfortable with "just the family."

Value Your Pastor

This subject has been discussed on nearly every page of this book, so it is only necessary here to note that a healthy congregational self-image depends upon the love and concern a congregation shows for its minister. Often pastoral relationship is a microcosm of the way persons in the congregation treat each other. A congregation that respects and cares for its spiritual leader feels good about itself. On the contrary, a church that takes advantage of its shepherd feels guilty and small. Laypeople need to be sentries on constant lookout for anything that might hinder the effectiveness of their pastor or send a signal to a watching world that they have carelessly treated God's anointed leader.

Remember Ownership

Never forget that your church belongs to Christ. Charles Colson summarizes this point well when he reminds us:

> The church is not a democracy and never can be. We can change rules and practices and sing new hymns and use different styles of worship. We can change forms, but not our foundations. For the church is authoritarian. It is ruled over by Christ the Head and governed by a constitution that cannot be ignored or amended.[3]

All church leaders can chuckle in agreement with Hilaire Belloc's remark on the subject: "The church must be in God's hands because, seeing the people who have run it, it couldn't possibly have gone on existing if there weren't some help from above."[4] Rejoice in the reality that the church is the personal possession of Christ.

HOW WOULD YOU RATE YOUR CHURCH?

Now that we have walked through these simple but significant ideas about improving your church's self-concept, how would you rate your congregation? Remember, your answers indicate whether or not your church is effective and alive or just another church among many others.

We urge you, as a leader in your congregation, to sit down with other decision-making team members and use these helps to evaluate your congregation. If you pass the review process with flying colors, cheer your church. If improvements are needed, get started now. So much depends upon someone's taking decisive action to move ahead.

In Exodus 14, the children of Israel were in disarray as they fled from Egypt, and Moses was downtrodden. They were not feeling too good about themselves or their future. At that moment God stepped in and commanded Moses to move on. Moses relayed the message to the people: "Do not be afraid. Stand firm and you will see the deliverance the LORD will bring you today. . . . The LORD will fight for you!" (vv. 13-14).

We urge every church leader to go forward. When it is dark, look for the light. When it is daytime, look for the cloud of promise. The Lord God is with you. He offers all the power at His command, and that is more than you will need.

Consider what former United States Senate Chaplain Richard Halverson had to say about the posture of a church: "The church that Christ is building confronts the world, not by cleverness or wisdom, not by programs or methods or institutions. The church Christ is building confronts the world in the very power of God himself in the life of the believers."[5] The chaplain is right—our strength is in God.

It is an awesome truth: Building great churches means building great Christians. When this happens, the church becomes a gathering place of eternally and spiritually significant people. That gives every congregation everlasting relevance and makes every believer a "somebody." What a strong self-image this truth creates for every congregation in every setting around the world.

RENEWAL STRATEGIES FOR LAY LEADERS: HOW TO MAKE SURE YOUR CHURCH IS HOLY AND HEALTHY

1. Identify what God wants His Church to be in the world.
2. Identify and address the causes of low self-image such as poor location, bad reputation, lack of purpose and uninspired leadership.

3. Celebrate your church's unique features.

4. Build congregational confidence.

5. Risk taking the gospel to the cutting edge of society.

6. Find happy ways to resolve differences.

7. Take care of your congregation's financial needs but also cultivate a healthy generosity toward others.

8. Define and communicate your congregation's priorities.

9. Remind decision makers that every tradition was once an innovation.

10. Emphasize who really owns the church.

Notes

1. Samuel T. Kamaleson, personal letter to H. B. London, n.d.
2. Vance Havner, *In Tune with Heaven* (Grand Rapids, MI: Baker Books, 1990), p. 57.
3. Charles Colson, *The Body* (Dallas, TX: Word, 1992), p. 187.
4. Hilaire Belloc, quoted in Malcolm Muggeridge, *Confessions of a Twentieth-Century Pilgrim* (San Francisco, CA: Harper and Row, 1988), p. 139.
5. Richard Halverson, *The Living Body* (Gresham, OR: Vision House, 1994), p. 48.

Each one should use whatever gift he has received to serve others, faithfully administering God's grace in its various forms. If anyone speaks, he should do it as one speaking the very words of God. If anyone serves, he should do it with the strength God provides, so that in all things God may be praised through Jesus Christ.

1 PETER 4:10-11

PASTORS UNDER FIRE

WHAT SHOULD LAY LEADERS DO FOR THEIR FAVORITE PASTOR?

God, the great head of the Church,
> *I rejoice in the privilege of serving You through*
> *Your Church.*
> *Help our congregation, especially me, to cherish*
> *our spiritual leader more.*
> *We are grateful for our pastor's ministry.*
> *Thanks for calling our minister into Your service.*
> *Thanks, too, for calling our pastor to this place.*
> *Enable us to serve together—pastor and people—*
> *as if this were our last day or, better still, as if it*
> *were our first day.*
> *Amen.*

Sometimes serving as a pastor resembles Marcie's comical experiences in a Peanuts cartoon. She felt frustration when she tried to kick a football, because it fell on her head rather than floating downfield. She observed dejectedly, "When I kicked the ball, my glasses, my sock, and my shoe all flew off, and the ball hit me on the head."

Then she added an aside to Charlie Brown, "Football is a humorous game, isn't it, sir?"

Charlie Brown replied philosophically, "Humorous if you aren't serious about football."[1]

Ministry can be like that, too. Urgent demands coupled with slow results might be humorous if your pastor were not serious about representing Christ.

Today's pastors face crises unknown to other occupational groups. Contemporary parish ministry has become an emotional and spiritual land mine, ready to explode at any second. Demands are up; credibility is down. Suspicions are up; needs are up. Comrades are going AWOL at the front lines—sometimes they choose to become gas station attendants, therapists or carpenters instead of pastors. Meanwhile, many ministry training programs seem out of touch with parish, community and global realities. Larger hordes of dysfunctional people in the general population mean more emotionally crippled and relationally wounded people attend every church. Time and financial commitments keep getting more complicated. Volunteer lay leaders have less time to devote to the church. Earning enough money to meet rising living standards steals time from marriage and parental obligations. As a result, people expect more from a pastor's preaching, teaching, counseling and financial leadership. In a nutshell, the pastor is expected to fill all gaps created by a fast-paced, demanding culture.

THE MAILBAG TELLS A SAD STORY

Hundreds of letters addressed to Focus on the Family describe excruciatingly painful situations many pastors face. Here is a sample:

Dear H. B.: We'll be leaving the pastoral ministry once and for all in a few days. My family, especially my wife, cannot continue to survive the continuous stress of a church. I must leave pastoral ministry to remain faithful to God—maybe to save my soul. I have felt so constrained by the politics of the whole thing that I have not been a spiritual leader. I am a title holder. I do pastoral things. If I were to describe my church and denomination, I would say "spiritually dead, yet physically functioning." Pulling the right strings without making waves has been a killer. I can say that if someone were not praying for us, I would walk away to call myself an atheist. In spite of people and problems, the Lord Jesus Christ has preserved my faith. . . . Since speaking with my denomination leaders and fellow pastors, I find that five out of eight have been or are living under the same oppression we're leaving. My heart goes out to them. It amazes me that they, too, do not go on to other ministries or secular work.[2]

The following phrases indicate the spirit of the letter and describe this pastor's broken dreams:

- I cannot survive the continued stress.
- I must leave to be faithful to God.
- I have become a title holder rather than a spiritual leader.
- My church is spiritually dead but physically functional.
- Pulling the right strings has been a killer.
- Without prayers, I would have walked away an atheist.

Is it possible that your pastor faces similar frustrations? If it is, then why not do something to improve the situation? In the contemporary church, lay leaders are called to come alongside pastors to facilitate their spiritual renewal and emotional wholeness.

Like Moses, pastors need someone to hold up their hands in battle and to perform lesser duties so that they can give themselves to eternal issues. Ministers need someone to free them from minutiae so that they can do what God has called them to do. Ministers need someone to befriend them, to care for them and to lovingly keep them accountable.

When pastors are at risk, the Church of Jesus Christ is under siege. As we talk with pastors, we hear cries of sadness and frustration from their hearts. They want to be servant leaders to help transform lives, to make a significant difference—but they feel stymied by pressures. And they are bone-weary after facing so many constraints and frustrations.

Sometimes we want to take a pastor's hand to assure her everything will be fine. But we are not convinced that everything will be fine until the Church recognizes the problems and local congregations do something to improve the way they treat their pastors. We are not sure it will be fine until all believers see that we are in this battle together—pastors, lay leaders and church members. This is a powerful team that can do great things for God. But if we are to win the world, we must have pastors who possess spiritual strength. We need fulfilled pastors who love the ministry. We need pastors who know that they have a laity that is committed to helping them. We must have pastors who are provided with the best possible opportunities to do ministry.

UNREALISTIC EXPECTATIONS

Look at the collision of confusing expectations from an advertisement written by a pulpit committee and published in a magazine for pastors:

Seeking an exceptional, committed individual for unique ministry in central [name of state] willing to help us survive and reach our potential and be an active participant in maintaining a strong Christian witness with a stable congregation of 40 members, all ages. A national park is close, golf and fishing are convenient. Other recreational opportunities are within easy driving distance. Rock hounding paradise. This is a challenge. Prospective pastors must be willing to experience new perspectives, different culture, and great satisfaction. Tent-making or part-time position.[3]

Think of the unrealistic demands in that advertisement: Come take secular employment as a tent-making pastor, so you can serve 40 church members. We want a pastor who can help us survive, fulfill our potential and maintain a strong witness. All of these expectations are to be accomplished by a person who welcomes new perspectives and a different culture. After reading the advertisement, one skeptical minister remarked: "Too bad they can't find someone who walks on water, flies without wings and hunts antelope for food."[4]

Contrast that advertisement with what ministers consider their most important priorities. A recent study showed that pastors value a solid marriage, the challenge of preaching, a sense of calling to the ministry and fulfillment from giving pastoral care as the most significant satisfactions in their lives. Yet these concerns apparently are low priorities for the pastoral search committee that placed the advertisement seeking a pastor for a church of 40 people. No wonder we have so much confusion in so many places!

MEET THE PASTORS

When a congregation and a pastor have diametrically different viewpoints, friction is often the result. To build bridges between pastors who feel under fire and congregations that sense confusion, let's meet several committed pastors. We have taken the liberty to change their names to protect the innocent, but their situations are indeed real.

By getting acquainted with these servants of the church, you can see how ministry has become very complex. In this chapter we unfold the stories of pastors who need parishioners to help them renew their sagging spirits. Each one has a different but common problem to overcome. These examples hopefully will show us all that lay leaders must help pastors design strategies to meet their personal challenges and at the same time respond with new energy and imagination to the ever-changing demands of a church. The effectiveness of a pastor's ministry is often shaped by how lay leaders handle these issues.

Jack Brownstone: Walk-on-Water Syndrome

In ministerial training programs Jack learned that Christ and the Church deserve high-level competency. Then, he graduated and took his first church assignment. That is where we meet him.

Pastor Brownstone tries to apply a standard of excellence to everything he does. Each day he works hard to become a gifted speaker, effective administrator, skilled fund-raiser, competent counselor, sensitive listener and faithful pastor. He proves himself to be a highly competent minister, even though he is just a beginner.

In these early months, he experiences some internal conflict, a common malady for first-time pastors. When leaders such as Jack conscientiously try to do ministry, they sometimes have difficulty delegating assignments. They fear that the work will not get done or that they will get mediocre results. As a result, Jack does too much by himself.

Meanwhile, church members expect Jack to walk on water, preach like Jesus and pray like Paul. They assume that he has ESP,

can be at more than one place at the same time and has a model
marriage with flawless children. Some church members have
become annoyed when they discover that no human being can
live up to what they demand. Nearly two-thirds of all pastors feel
immobilized by congregational expectations such as these.[4] They
feel trapped by expectations—their own and those of others.

This walk-on-water syndrome sometimes hurts ministers in
another way. Affirmed by their members as being superpastors,
they begin to believe all the nice things parishioners say about
them. They conclude that they can do no wrong, that no one else
can do everything as well as they can and that they deserve every
privilege they can get. In the process, it is easy to become obnox-
ious and ego-centered.

The apostle Peter demonstrated how walking on water was
impossible for human beings. He also quickly discovered that
a person can drown if he takes his eyes off Christ (see Matt.
14:28-31).

Lay leaders should not expect pastors to be experts at everything. To foster happy, productive relationships, pastors and
church members should develop an accurate awareness of what
needs to be done and who can do it. No pastor should be expected to do any task a layperson can do effectively.

Tom Addams: Moral Crusader

Troubled by the moral decline in contemporary society, Tom
Addams can be counted on to preach about vanishing absolutes.
He often thunders prophetic utterances from his pulpit about
murder, lying, stealing and the worship of the modern idols of
secularism. Recently he preached against adultery, including the
emotional kind. He was biblical, prophetic and quite specific.

A huge uproar followed—a kind of emotional earthquake.
Many people in the church were furious but did not want Tom to
know how much his preaching had bothered them. Tom, however,

recognized their displaced anger which emerged as outrage over a minor issue that stemmed from an event that, from a distance, appeared to be unrelated.

When Tom saw the anger, he became confused. He asked himself: *Should I deal with what I think are "real issues" or try to put out tiny fires?* In his bewilderment, Tom sought the help of a respected lay leader. After the conversation, Tom became even more confused over his duty to declare truths from Scripture and the need to keep complainers happy. He did not see how he could do both.

> *Many Christians have moved from measuring their lives by Scripture to doing what is right in their own eyes.*

It is a tough call. At a time when most Americans say there is no such thing as absolute truth, it is difficult to preach about keeping the Ten Commandments—in many places they are now regarded as the 10 suggestions. What was once considered absolute truth is now considered mere opinion. Many Christians have moved from measuring their lives by Scripture to doing what is right in their own eyes. The contemporary crisis in our churches and communities is proof that "there is a way that seems right to a man, but in the end it leads to death" (Prov. 14:12). Meanwhile, society dies a miserable suicide because its members have given up on virtues such as self-control, compassion, tolerance, faith, integrity, morality and respect for authority. No civilization can survive such loss.

Greg Brookes: New Breed, Bivocational

Greg Brookes, age 30, and his wife, Carrie, serve a 50-year-old, 70-member church in a town of 8,000 in the heartland. They have two children, ages 4 and 6.

For years before they came, the church had had pastors who were willing to live below the poverty line while members enjoyed a middle-class lifestyle. Such a sacrifice by the Brookes's family was expected; no one questioned the arrangement. Whenever former pastors had had a personal economic crisis, they took part-time jobs in a grocery store owned by a church member or moved to another church. The situation changed when Greg arrived, although the church's financial compensation did not.

Greg has computer-drafting skills that allow him to do free-lance work. He sends his projects by modem to his employer's office in a distant city. He usually works about 20 hours a week in his home, which produces more income than the church pays him. As a result, he lives a comfortable middle-class lifestyle, drives the kind of car he wants and clothes his family in a fashion similar to that of his parishioners.

After a time, the church offered Greg a $3,000 annual raise provided he worked full-time for the church. That would have brought his cash salary from the church to a grand total of $13,000 per year, plus housing and utilities. When Greg declined, several old-time church members questioned his commitment to ministry—without considering his and his wife's educational loans, which amounted to more than $25,000 when they graduated from seminary. Neither did the questioners think about the future college funds needed for the children. Nor did they think to compare their standard of living to his.

This has become a touchy situation, so no one in the official decision-making group discusses it with Greg. Nonetheless, a continuous murmuring can be heard throughout the congregation. Deep down, even the critics know they would rather have Greg as pastor on a bivocational basis than someone else who would be willing to scrimp along with low wages.

No one knows where this confusion between Greg and this church will lead. But just below the surface, there are several hard issues that all lay leaders need to consider concerning their minister's salary.

Can a pastor maintain a middle-class standard of living on the current compensation package?

Does the church want its pastor to live at the poverty line?

Can a pastor repay from his current income level his educational expenses incurred in ministry training?

How much latitude should a low-paying church allow its pastor when he is doing his ministry as well or better than a full-time minister of more limited ability?

It would be wise to discuss economic issues in a nonjudgmental way with your pastor. As you talk you will come to see the challenges from his point of view.

Unlike many professionals, pastors are limited in the ways they can earn extra income. Thus, they often feel locked in by their present economic situation. Because their pay package has been low for so many years, most ministers need more than a token annual increase or a cost-of-living raise. Someone needs to champion significant raises as the rule for pastors, not the exception. Being locked in to financial prisons makes pastors weary, causes them to lose the challenge for their work and tempts them to quit so that they can become better providers for their families. Most churches could give their pastor a significant salary increase next Sunday if some lay leader challenged the congregation to do so.

Craig Eaves: Emotionally Exhausted

Craig serves a growing suburban congregation of mostly new believers. For the most part, the members had been employed in factories in the Great Lakes region for years. With the dawning of the information age and technological advances, many factories have closed, displacing thousands of workers. Some lost their jobs, others had to take lower-paying positions, and others wondered if they would be the next to be unemployed.

Many new converts were attracted to Craig's church because it offers peace, wholeness and stability. Some newcomers had dysfunctional pasts, including abuse, broken marriages and drug and alcohol addictions. Old-timers in the church have no frame of reference for understanding these problems or the massive increase these needs create in a pastor's workload. Although it is seldom mentioned, effective evangelism increases demands on a faithful pastor's workload—the more people who find Christ, the more ministers will have to serve people who bring incredible baggage with them.

In addition to the problems of his church members, Craig also carries scars from his own emotionally fractured childhood. His wife, Mary, also has hurts—her father deserted their family when she was 6. Trying to be a Christian family is hard work for Craig and Mary. They consider such a struggle important to their personal wholeness, and they believe a good marriage serves as a model of what a Christian home should be. Craig and Mary have a deep commitment to each other and to their children, but they are forced to deal with their own emotional impairments even as they work to help heal the wounded people in the congregation.

At one point, Mary told a mentoring friend that she and Craig felt emotionally spent because they faced so many problems in church members' lives. She also confessed that they felt terrorized by the emotional and relationship crises that they observed in the lives of pastoral peers. Mary sees no relief in sight. Taking the strength of the Lord into dysfunctional lives is rewarding but fatiguing work.

What can lay leaders do to help their pastors carry these heavy duties?

Understand your pastor. When he seems preoccupied or pensive, try to understand that he may be dealing with confusing issues concerning someone's hurts. The greatest demands are often issues that are the most confidential.

Encourage your pastor to take a break. Help her take a break from her duties by inviting her to lunch or coffee without discussing church work. Invite your pastor to a social or athletic event that will help her set aside the needs of hurting people for a few hours.

Help troubled people in your church. Become a listener or leaning post to someone who has problems. Often a simple affirmation, such as "I'm glad to see you growing in Christ," encourages an individual to get his focus on the Lord. When you do this, you give an overworked pastor some needed relief.

Offer to become a spiritual mentor to new converts. Teach them how to pray. Show them how to read the Bible. Encourage them in every possible way. Keep close enough so that they are willing to share the frustrations of their pilgrimage with you. Like raising an infant, caring for a new convert is often frustrating and time consuming. In spite of the demands, however, your efforts usually pay off and keep the new convert from demanding too much emotional support from the pastor. Everyone wins in such an effort: You help the new convert, you relieve the pastor, and, in the process, you enjoy the satisfaction such ministry produces.

Rich Shields: AWOL

Rich Shields fit the traditional image of a good pastor. Faithful, loyal, trustworthy and steady, he apparently loved everybody and was loved in return.

Yet one day he mysteriously disappeared, leaving his wife and nearly grown children and deserting his church—an AWOL pastor. Friends and family members could not think of any logical reason for his disappearance—perhaps he might have experienced a blackout or was trying to run away from some dark secret, they wondered. Because he was so faithful, some feared Rich was a victim of foul play. No one could believe he would walk off without telling anyone.

After a few days, his wife, Rachel, filed a missing person's report. An all-points police bulletin was issued across several states. No one came up with any clues, because Rich did not use his checking account or credit cards. No one heard from him for nearly six months. Finally, Rich called his wife from a public phone a thousand miles away, telling her to get a divorce and spend their combined assets. He said he wanted a new life in a new place with a new identity. He took a new name and applied for a new Social Security card. He wanted a job dealing with things, rather than with people.

Rich's story is true but, thankfully, not common. Nonetheless, many ministers have left a thousand times in their minds. Many others stay but have quietly lost heart for the work.

How does this happen? Trivial functions become too demanding. Apathy among lay leaders suffocates. Rich did nearly everything in his church, and the people let him. He cut grass, painted buildings, preached sermons, deposited offerings, visited the sick, raised his kids under the critical scrutiny of church members and tried to keep his wife happy.

Rich played by the rules, staying in the game for 20 years. In a phone interview since leaving, he said:

> I couldn't cope with secular values in the church and felt responsible to correct moral chaos outside the church. I left because I could not make a difference, so why keep

trying? I became weary of those who think a minister does not work when he is bivocational. For years I paid most of the bills at my churches from my vocational job. It seemed my sacrifice was wasted, so I saw no point in continuing.

Consider Rick's perspective—he did not quit because he gave up on God but because he thought the cause was no longer worthy of his investment. What if he is right?

Members of decision-making groups must realize that some discouraged pastors would quit today if they had another way to support themselves. Lay leaders can prevent much of this pain by giving attention to the care and feeding of their pastors. Ask yourself what you can do to help your ministers find fulfillment in their work. Seldom do pastors burn out or quit during a time of spiritual revival; it usually happens during shallow, tough times when the work is frustrating and the results are negligible.

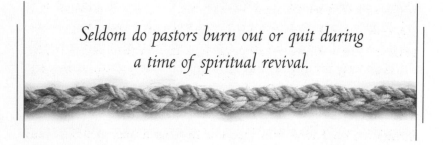

Seldom do pastors burn out or quit during a time of spiritual revival.

Ask yourself and others often if your church is doing the main business of Christ for the right reasons. Does your congregation deserve a leader who has been called by God to give years of his life to its ministry? Or is your church a Kingdom outpost that expects pastors to keep the store, maintain routines and keep everyone happy—including the spiritually immature and fringe folks? Is your fellowship a place where a pastor will look back in 20 years and think every sacrifice was worth it? Will he remember spiritual breakthroughs you experienced together and be able to recall those who were rescued from the despair of their sinful lives?

Wayne Charleston: The Marriage and Ministry Competition

College sweethearts, Wayne and Jan married on graduation day. As they moved on to seminary life, Jan immediately started feeling that Wayne's studies and their marriage were in competition with each other. Wayne, too, felt divided between his studies, in which he wanted to do well, and his marriage, in which he wanted to be the best husband any woman ever had. This competition continued into the pastorate.

Wayne became a ministry workaholic. He fooled himself into believing he could do something significant for God if only he put in the time. As a result, Wayne and Jan grew further apart. At this time, she worked two days each week as a nurse at the nearby hospital, giving the rest of her energies to being a homemaker and good mother to their two children. Their emotional and physical distance was obvious to everyone around them, but outsiders thought it was the normal chemistry of their relationship.

Both of them were alarmingly vulnerable to outside emotional attachments. Soon Wayne became sexually involved with a female whom he had been counseling. He never intended that an innocent flirtation would take him that far. But his moral weakness had started with a thousand smaller issues that he had allowed in his ministry and marriage. He simply could not see his need for balance. As a result, ministry is now over for Wayne and Jan.

Of course, infidelity is wrong. It annihilates pastoral credibility and sabotages everything a pastor has accomplished for God. It violates people, breaks up marriages and crushes children.

Can lay leaders do something to prevent a pastor's infidelity? Every church decision-making group can encourage its pastor to view the importance of a healthy marriage and how it relates to being a whole person. Every church needs a whole pastor preaching from its pulpit. And every church needs a beautiful model of Christian marriage and family life lived out in front of them. Thus, every effort at building a great marriage is a great investment in ministry.

Naturally, some unmarried pastors serve with devotion and biblical piety. They too must follow the biblical directive that "among you there must not be even a hint of sexual immorality, or of any kind of impurity, or of greed, because these are improper for God's holy people" (Eph. 5:3, *NIV*). Whether pastors are single or married, they must lead the way in emotional and spiritual wholeness. Their congregations have a right to expect it and that is the kind of living the Lord honors.

Lay leaders do their congregations an important favor by encouraging their pastor to find balance between marriage and ministry. Encourage him to take the time and effort it requires to maintain a healthy marriage. If needed, raise money outside regular giving channels so that your ministry couple can get away together; it will be a worthwhile investment.

Although no one can take responsibility for the strength of the pastor's marriage, church leaders can help by means of affirmation, influence and encouragement. Remember three important facts: Pastors are alarmingly vulnerable to outside emotional temptations during times of hopelessness; a good marriage is an important strength for effective ministry; and a church seldom completely recovers from a pastor's infidelity.

God never intended ministry and marriage to be in competition. When such competition exists, someone must change it.

Toby Mohr: Frustrated

After 10 years of serving a tiny three-generation family church in a small midwestern town, Toby moved to California and became pastor of a 200-member congregation.

His new church had a well-balanced lineup of ministries. However, during Toby's first year there, he encountered a consumer mentality and what he considered to be a severe lack of loyalty among many in his flock. Two families left because the teens liked the youth pastor at a nearby church. Three unmarried members decided to go to a church that had a larger ministry for singles. Two key leaders wanted to know why their church could not have a contemporary Saturday night service like the 3,000-member megachurch around the corner.

If all of that were not enough, Toby wanted to scream when a newly retired couple who had been members of the church's core group started looking for a new place to worship because they "were not being fed."

The consumer mentality sweeping through the church is driving some pastors crazy. It is estimated that as many as 80 percent of all church membership gains in a recent year were the result of people leaving one church and joining another. Like choosing a dry cleaner, supermarket or mechanic, people shop around for a church. They too often consider the facilities, programs and personality of the preacher instead of the beliefs, doctrine and mission.

Sometimes believers move to another church without offering an explanation and with almost no reason. They find a better church nursery or more convenient parking near the church's front door, and off they go. They attend a concert by a big-name Christian band at a church across town and never return. Every loss fuels feelings of despair for the pastor, because relationships are so much a part of ministry.

Lay leaders can discourage member migration by conscientiously listening to concerns and doing something about them. Too often a pastor suggests improvements that are rejected by the decision-making group; these refusals are often the reason people leave. Stand alongside your pastor in these matters.

Encourage people to believe that they never need to go anywhere else, because this church loves them and wants to minister to them in every possible way. Create a church climate that nobody wants to leave.

Mike Wyley: Invisible Casualties

Handsome, outgoing and well dressed, Mike Wyley told me (Neil) his story while I shopped for a sport coat at a Kansas City men's store. When he discovered I was a friendly advocate for pastors, he told me about his unbelievable experience.

After scraping together enough money to finish seminary, Mike and his wife, Jill, took their first charge among loving people in a small church whose members knew that effective pastors did not stay long. This church had lots of experience affirming pastors, only to see them move on to a larger assignment in a year or two. Mike and Jill, just as the church leaders expected, followed the familiar pattern.

After six years at the new church and the addition of two children to the family, Jill reached a breaking point. One day she announced, "I am tired of the petty gossip about our family, so I'm leaving. You keep the kids. I want freedom."

Mike stayed on at the church for nearly a year, trying to be a single father and a pastor. The going was rough—he had to be mom and dad, clean the house, cook the meals, do laundry and try to shepherd his congregation. When Mike suggested that he leave, lay leaders agreed that it would not work for him to continue. Now he is among the church's invisible casualties, one of the walking wounded. He is one of the emotionally and spiritually afflicted and forgotten.

Most Sundays, Mike takes the children to a neighborhood church of a denomination different from the one he served in. He sells men's clothing during the week to earn a living and doubts whether he will ever return to the ministry. Even though he tries to view his former congregation in the best possible light, he sometimes feels bitterness toward them.

But someone is responsible for his plight. Do gossipers in his former church bear responsibility? Or does the fault belong to his wife? Or perhaps Mike lost his wife because he took his work too seriously. Or does someone else bear blame for stifling his idealism, perpetuating his poverty and invading his privacy?

Mike is one of the unobtrusive casualties most people do not think about when discussing the pastoral crises in our time. What will Mike feel in 15 years when he recalls his dreams of Christian service? What will his children remember, and what did they miss? And what about the loss to churches that could have benefited so much from Mike's ministry?

It is sad to hear a person say "I used to be a pastor, but it just didn't work out." What he means is "My dream died and someone killed it." Can the church continue to allow the wounded to die without heroic efforts to save them?

Lay leaders should do all that they can to keep Mike's situation from occurring in their churches. They should see to it that their pastor is cherished and that his family has what it needs. Someone in the leadership group can be chosen to be the pastor's ombudsman. A quiet, friendly, caring advocate will do wonders to keep a pastor encouraged and emotionally strong.

INSIDE A PASTOR'S WORLD

The people you have met in this chapter are flesh-and-blood pastors. They are an interesting and highly committed group who, because they usually are prepared to give a lifetime of service to Christ, are among the church's priceless possessions. Yet there is often a great deal of pain in their lives, some of which can be easily remedied by lay leaders.

Let's be sure we have a clear picture of the typical pastor's world today. Pastors in North America live in a realm that never stops, where the light never goes out and where the average workweek is between 55 and 75 hours. One in eight pastors is bivocational or multivocational, and 70 percent of their spouses work outside the home—meaning either or both hold down secular jobs as a way to keep themselves in ministry.

Pastors dwell in a world of the unfinished tyranny, where they cannot shut the door or walk out of the office. There is always another Bible study, sermon, phone call, committee, hospital call or home visit clamoring for attention. When someone dies, gets married or is hospitalized, the well-planned schedule has to be abandoned, appointments put off until later. Sometimes "later" is a long time away.

Pastors live in a world of guilt when they consider their families. Most want a Christ-exalting family life that models marriage and parenting for their congregation. But that is tough to accomplish when they often spend more time with other people's kids than they spend with their own and more time with adults other than with their spouse.

Pastors reside in a world of decreasing approval. Even though a pastor was once among the most revered people in our society, a recent Gallup poll shows that clergy are ranked 56 out of 100 admired professionals. When the Bakkers, Swaggarts and many lesser-known ministers fall morally or compromise their integrity, they not only destroy their credibility and hurt innocent people, they also have a negative impact on every brother and sister in ministry.

Pastors serve in a me-centered world in which church members and attendees are becoming more and more apathetic. By contrast, Jesus promised to build His Church so that the gates of hell would never prevail against it (see Matt. 16:18). Perhaps the passage might be paraphrased to say the "self-centered members of the Church cannot prevail against it." In a day of declining morality, it is becoming more difficult to speak the truth, even in church. So we grasp for new ways, new paradigms and new methods, and we forget the old mission and the everlasting message. In many corners of the Church, the gospel has been watered down. Some ministers doubt whether they can make a difference in times like these. Consequently, pastors who want their lives to count are asking if ministry is worth the effort.

When we look at a pastor's world through these lenses, the situation appears to be bleak—but we can change it. The present problem reminds us of a recent interview aired on a television show. The head of the trauma center at Parkland Hospital in Dallas was asked about the revoked federally mandated speed limits on freeways. The physician replied with anguish, "When speed limits are increased, our trauma cases will increase by at least twenty percent. I don't know who will care for those hurting, sick, dying people if we cannot find more doctors, more nurses, more budget. We're at capacity now most of the time—we just do not have a margin for all the increase."[5]

The doctor's comments sound similar to a diagnosis of the current situation in many churches. At a time when the world needs pastors more than ever, intentional action must be taken to encourage, renew, compensate and love pastors into greatness. We are losing ground in the clergy personnel pool with fewer recruits, forced resignations, increased early retirements and more pastors who are running in place and not getting anywhere.

Ultimately, the issue is spiritual, not vocational or cultural. The Church has in many ways become passionless. We are lukewarm. The Church sits powerless, like a shell without powder, looking the part but not making much difference. And as we sit and talk and pray and cry with pastors, they ask, "What do we have to do? What do we have to say? Where do we have to go? What extreme measures do we have to take?"

Can't the lay leaders of your church do something to help?
Can't *you* do something to make a difference?

RENEWAL STRATEGIES FOR LAY LEADERS: HOW TO LOWER THE RISKS YOUR PASTOR FACES

1. Create a counterculture, so your church is obviously different from the world.
2. Cherish your minister's Christlike character as a priceless asset.
3. Realize a church is at serious risk when its pastor is under fire.
4. Come alongside your pastor to facilitate renewal and achievement.
5. Do your part to keep your pastor from becoming a victim of ministry burnout.
6. Champion the cause of making congregational expectations reasonable.
7. Question or, if necessary, confront your pastor about his work schedule.
8. Understand when your pastor is pensive. She may be dealing with an overwhelming problem in someone's life.
9. Keep asking the decision-making group if your church is actually accomplishing the main business of Christ.
10. Try viewing all issues from our Lord's perspective.

Notes
1. Source unknown.
2. Anonymous, letter to H. B. London.

3. *Monday Morning Magazine*, n.d., n.p.
4. Anonymous, conversation with Neil Wiseman.
5. Source unknown.

For the church is not a human society of people
united by their natural affinities but the body of Christ,
in which all members, however different, must share the
common life, complementing and helping one another
precisely by their differences.

C. S. LEWIS, *THE QUOTABLE C. S. LEWIS*

CHAPTER 9

A Pastor's Bill of Rights

LIBERATING YOUR MINISTER TO GREATNESS

Holy God, the One who calls and sustains our minister,
    show us how
    to better encourage our pastor,
    to love our pastor better,
    to challenge our pastor to greatness,
    to follow our pastor, where You lead,
    to affirm our pastor's strengths and
    to pray for our pastor's continued empowerment.
    Amen.

A pastor's rights? You say that you have never heard of such a thing? What would a bill of rights include? Why is it necessary? And what would it accomplish?

Consider what a bill of rights is intended to accomplish. Check any encyclopedia to learn details such as James Madison's leadership role in formulating the document, for the purpose of ensuring ratification of the United States Constitution by the States. Concepts found in the Bill of Rights are deeply rooted in the Bible and in Greek and Roman civilizations. Historical personalities such as John Locke, John Milton, John Stuart Mill and Thomas Paine all had a strong part in shaping the United States Bill of Rights, which went into effect in 1791. The Bill of Rights has protected Americans' fundamental liberties for more than 200 years. Similar documents guarantee rights in Great Britain, France, Canada and the United Nations.

When a pastoral bill of rights is suggested, several concerns come to mind immediately. Rights, on the most basic level, require responsible relationships between two or more parties. That's an important part of this whole picture. For example, civil rights guarantee protection for citizens. Children's rights mandate the responsibilities of parents and government to children. Patients' rights charge physicians, medical staff, insurance providers and hospitals to have responsibility for sick people. In Western civilizations, workers' rights ensure employees a right to be paid, to be provided with adequate tools and to have a safe working environment. Rights grow out of responsibilities based on relationships. Thus, responsible relationships between pastors and parishioners are the cornerstone for formulating a pastor's bill of rights.

Laypersons also have rights in church. Everyone understands that lay believers have rights of full acceptance, hearing the gospel, faithful ministry from a pastor and an opportunity for fulfilling service. They have family rights, because they were adopted into God's family at the time of their conversion. These rights are based on Scripture, redemptive relationships, standard practices throughout Church history and previous experiences in a particular congregation.

Rights between a pastor and a congregation, however, are unique among all human associations. These rights are not like those between employer and employee. These rights are different from pay-for-service relationships such as doctors or lawyers have with patients or clients. Neither are pastoral rights a legally guaranteed right, such as equal opportunity, airline safety or clean water. Consequently, because a pastor's rights are unique, they are sometimes forgotten or ignored.

Let's discuss those rights so that we can understand them and make full use of them. What obligations does a congregation owe a pastor? What rights should every congregation give a pastor? What entitlements go with a call to ministry? Closely connected to these concerns is an even more important question—can a congregation be an authentic church without granting rights of leadership to its pastor?

This book has been written to build bridges of relationships between lay leaders and clergy. For churches that already possess wholesome connections with their pastors, we have tried to fortify, encourage and celebrate those relationships. For others, we have suggested ways to circumvent problems before they start. For those congregations experiencing difficulties, we have offered strategies for restoration and renewal.

In summary form we want to restate the key issues in a pastor's bill of rights. Although many of these ideas have already been presented, we feel that their importance merits a second look. Though John D. Rockefeller probably did not have churches in mind, his advice applies with incredible accuracy: "Every right implies a responsibility; every opportunity, an obligation; every possession, a duty."[1]

I. THE RIGHT TO DREAM

As a young pastor, I (H. B.) remember sharing my dreams with my first congregation. Like many churches, the congregation had several lay leaders who seemed determined to sabotage my vision. Try to see the picture clearly. It was my first church. I was young with a new seminary degree in my hand. My dreams were simple, but I had a vision for what I believed God could do in my first assignment.

Sadly, a small group of experienced footdraggers stymied my dreams. No board member wanted to challenge these power brokers because of their contentious spirit. As often happens, these controllers were neither spiritually minded nor forward thinking. Rather, they were self-centered people who wanted control so that they could have prominence. Controllers usually want to rule or ruin. These leaders wanted to keep everything as it was so they could be in charge; they were rashly wrong in seeking to keep the church in a status quo mode.

An important warning should be sounded and heeded. Laypersons must be aware of the possible consequences before they allow themselves to get stuck in this quagmire. God judges those who sabotage the work of the congregation. Though it may be a hard lesson for those addicted to power, the church is no plaything. The Church is an eternal vine of the Lord's planting—the Body of Christ, the family of God, the people of God. The Church is God's instrument for saving a lost world. Therefore, those who turn a church into a social power base defile Christ's mission for His Church. Those who thwart God's purpose stand in judgment. Let controllers everywhere carefully consider the serious repercussions before they thwart the God-given dream of an anointed leader.

That is exactly what happened in the church where I served. New people attended. Lives were transformed. Human miracles of God's grace happened; however, people were not impressed by the power brokers' base but by what God was doing in their lives. The congregation was like those standing on the edge of Jesus' ministry as He worked miracles. Some were in the crowd because of their spiritual struggles and hungers. Others came looking for opportunities to shut down the gospel any way they could. However, the spiritual groundswell was so infectious for a period of time that power-hungry folks could not stop it. But they kept alert to every possible opportunity for causing mischief.

They tried to kill the dream by crucifying the leader. But they failed, because the dream lived on.

As a pastor shares God-given dreams, congregations begin seeing their church in a whole new way.

A similar thing happens today. As a pastor shares God-given dreams, congregations begin seeing their church in a whole new way. Then a crisis starts. As the Lord walks in the midst of His Church, power controllers stand in the shadows, undermining progress. In many cases, the pastor can't survive because controllers see to it that any step forward will seem too difficult or too expensive—even when it's not.

Think of the incredible losses that follow. Those who have been considering accepting Christ give up the church to those who want it, like a childish game of marbles on the school playground. Dreamers stop dreaming, or they become reluctant to share new dreams. Potential believers lose interest, sometimes for a lifetime. Pastors move. Controllers shrivel up spiritually, because they know they have wrecked the potential of their church. In the process, power brokers often see their children and grandchildren lose the faith. Meanwhile, these same controllers consider suspect every church that is showing progress and winning new people.

Dreams are fragile. Before you criticize another person's dream, remember this wisdom from an unknown sage: "It [a dream] can be killed by a sneer or a yawn; it can be stabbed to death by a quip and worried to death by a frown on the right person's brow."[2] That is serious stuff.

Here is a self-test to help you determine if you are a champion or killer of dreams:

- Do you encourage your pastor to dream?
- Are you a help or hindrance to your pastor's dream?
- Are you an affirmer or a foot dragger?
- Do you ask "Why not?" or "How come?" when you hear about your pastor's dream for your church?
- Do you pray that your pastor will be uniquely blessed with creative ways to touch people?
- Do you tell your pastor "Go for it!" or do you ride the spiritual bus with your foot on the brake?

The positive thinker Norman Vincent Peale challenged church leaders to "be a possibilitarian. No matter how dark things seem to be or actually are, raise your sights and see possibilities—always see them, for they're always there."[3] That is what your pastor needs from you. Not all dreams will work, but some will. Fruitful dreams will broaden your church's ministry and grow your pastor's soul. Meanwhile, you will find joy in becoming a dream cheerleader, and your faith in what God can do will flourish.

II. THE RIGHT TO PRIVACY

Compassion and availability make a pastor live in a glass house where the work is never finished but the welcome is expected to be warm at all times. For some inexplicable reason, churches—especially smaller fellowships—sometimes behave as if they own the pastor and his family.

Think of the intrusive situations you have heard of—or perhaps caused. Church leaders pry into a pastor's family matters. Board members question how a minister spends his money. One snoopy busybody pieced together bits of a torn-up letter from a pastor's wastebasket and started rumors. One congregation thought its pastor dressed too expensively, and the next church thought her dreadfully plain. Some criticize the minister's car—it's too new, too old, too red or too expensive. Some churches expect a minister's children to never act like children. It's a strange world in which the "privacy please" sign is seldom observed.

Responsible lay leaders should do all they can to respect the privacy of the pastoral family and encourage others to do the same. When a young pastor's wife wore a maternity dress for the first time, a gossiper remarked to a lay leader, "Well, it's about time. They've been married five years." The lay leader responded quietly, "They have as much right to privacy as you do." The reply quieted the gossiper for a few minutes or perhaps for a few hours—but probably not for long.

Since the nature of ministry requires a pastor to live in a glass house, allow him the opportunity to pull down the shades and shut the world out just like other people do. Allow your minister an occasional time of family togetherness or marriage privacy as well as isolated hours for digging into the deepest realities of godliness. A German proverb shines light on the need for privacy between a pastor and his congregation: "A hedge between keeps friendships green." The hedge is a respect for privacy. A great pastor finds a near-equal balance of availability and privacy. Both should be respected and honored.

How does privacy look for a pastor? It is often nothing more than the simple satisfaction everyone else enjoys in everyday living. Privacy means uninterrupted meals, time with family members, time to stare into space, time to watch TV, time to pray, time to sit on the front stoop with a child and watch the world go by, or time to recover from Sunday's strains. Here is some perspective from former Archbishop of Canterbury Geoffrey Fisher, "There is a sacred realm of privacy for every pastor where he makes his own choices and decisions—a place of his own essential rights and liberties into which the church, generally speaking, must not intrude."[4] Fisher is right. Every minister needs a space where the church does not intrude. Give your pastor privacy as part of helping him be a fulfilled human being.

Urge your pastor to let the congregation know specifics regarding his family mealtimes, his day off and his family devotional times. Since many pastors might be reticent about announcing such preferences, lay leaders can share this information during pastor appreciation events, or it could be printed in Sunday bulletins or weekly newsletters as a communication from lay leaders. Help fellow church members understand that a pastor's home and study is where a minister goes to pray, study, think, unwind, relax and gain perspective—a place for refueling before going among the people again.

The essence of a pastor's work means that an evening or weekend to regroup is seldom available. Saturday and Sunday are a pastor's busy time to be with people and lead the church in worship—a weekend off almost never happens. Surveys show that pastors average less than two nights per week at home. Consequently, family time is always at a premium.

For these reasons, concerned lay leaders should sometimes question a pastor about how much time he spends with spouse and children. Encourage your minister to spend quality time with the most important people in his life. Help your pastor protect his limited privacy. Lead a charge to help your pastor take more time away from the church. A pastor's time away does not cost—it pays. A well-rested pastor with a balanced schedule always serves a church better over the long haul and will be a more well-rounded person.

Ask these questions as part of the continuing self-test:

- Do you or the decision-making group at your church make unreasonable demands on your pastor?
- Do you take liberties when arranging for a minister's living quarters?
- Do you defend the pastor's family when others question lifestyle issues?
- Do you ask your pastor tough accountability questions regarding her schedule and quality time with family?

III. The Right to Adequate Income

As an old joke goes, a layman once prayed, "Lord, You keep the pastor humble and we'll keep him poor." Though this may not have actually happened, it nearly always elicits a nervous chuckle because it contains a measure of truth. As everyone knows, pastors are seldom paid enough. The sad reality is that many churches could pay better with a little extra effort, but they do not try. Few churches ever have felt squeezed economically in order to give a generous raise to their pastor.

It is no secret that a pastor, or pastor's spouse, is often forced by economic necessity to be employed in the secular workplace, so the pastor can stay in the ministry. Let that fact sink in. Because of limited income, many ministers' spouses feel responsible to furnish economic safety nets that keep the minister in the service of the church.

Such sacrifice should be cherished and never wasted. Laypeople must take the lead to see their pastor is appropriately compensated, because ministerial support is every congregation's first financial obligation. No pastor should have to move to another church for financial reasons, but it happens every week. Though other reasons for leaving are politely given, some ministers have been "starved out." Sometimes this means controllers have withheld their giving to force a pastor's resignation.

Surveys show the average pastor needs an immediate annual increase of $2,000 to $8,000. Contrary to what some people think, money matters for ministers are not mysterious or hard to understand. Church decision-making groups sometimes act as if ministers don't understand costs of inflation, auto operations, sports shoes for teenagers, college tuition, professional books and respectable clothing. Like every other family, there has to be enough money to meet such needs.

One of the things lay leaders can do is to consider ways to help lessen a minister's "worry factor." Few pastors are in ministry for financial gain. Most feel called by God. At a life-changing crossroad, they answered a call from God to the Christian ministry, knowing there would be sacrifices. This commitment is "for better or for worse." Though pastors do not often complain about money, they worry about whether things will ever be different financially. They worry about college bills for the children and retirement costs. They need your help to alleviate the worry factor.

Lay leaders can help decrease the worry factor by occasionally asking a minister "Pastor, how are you doing financially?" Then listen and do something about it. If you don't ask the question, who will? And if you don't follow through on possible solutions, how will the situation ever improve?

Here are some more self-test questions for lay leaders:

- Do you know the average compensation of pastors in your community? Rejoice if your church pays more and take action if your church pays less.
- Do you know if your pastor has outstanding debt related to tuition bills from Bible college or seminary? Why not lead your church to help underwrite a portion of

those expenses as long as your pastor serves your congregation?

- Does your decision-making group review your pastor's compensation twice each year? In your decisions, be sure to consider car allowance, retirement benefits, salary raises, Social Security and health and dental insurance.
- Do you regularly consider the pastor's housing? If the church owns a parsonage, maintenance costs should be included in the budget. Members of a congregation can take as much pride in their pastor's housing as they take in their church facilities or their own homes.

IV. THE RIGHT TO CONTINUAL PROFESSIONAL DEVELOPMENT

Ministry, unlike other professions, is self-directed. A pastor lives with his own ideas, hears his own voice and serves the same people week after week. The physician is different because he or she consults with colleagues on a daily basis at the hospital; some are involved in partnership practices, so they have constant contact with others in their profession. Lawyers often work in combined law practices and have frequent conversations with accountants, physicians, judges and civic authorities. Teachers enjoy daily contact with fellow teachers and principals to help them keep their skills sharp and to test their conclusions. But because most pastors have almost none of these associations, they need opportunities for professional dialogue and continued development.

Many clergy, having been out of Bible college and seminary for years, are frighteningly out of touch with contemporary church trends and changes in society. They are at perilous disadvantage. One pastor wrote recently, "I just don't have what it takes to go with all the changes I see on the horizon of the church. What do I do?"

And this pastor is not alone. Studies show the words "inadequate" and "confused" pop up whenever pastors are asked to describe their ministry—a predictable result of doing ministry in isolation with the same people for an extended time. Such isolation leads to ministerial monotony, professional boredom and emotional burnout. The result is an unimaginative sameness in ministry.

Everything is changing, including us. Christian researcher George Barna believes our culture redefines itself twice every 10 years. That means the surroundings and atmosphere of ministry are significantly different from how they have ever been before. As a result, the way we do church needs to keep changing too. Meanwhile, many pastors do not understand how to change or why innovation is necessary. Many even argue that the church must stay the same, since the redemptive work of God is changeless. The trick, of course, is to know the difference between the unchanging message and changing methodologies.

The toughest part of developing an awareness to make these distinctions is that many pastors have no frame of reference or formal training for making needed changes. To help pastors understand their environment and maximize ministry to contemporary people, they need frequent opportunities to update their skills and renew their methods. Without these opportunities, the church will probably become increasingly more outdated and less relevant in the eyes of the world.

Decision-making groups must make more development opportunities available so that pastors can better understand their times. But how can it be done? It usually starts by providing money to attend development events, followed by a serious commitment on a minister's part to participate in such events.

A generous allowance should be built into a congregation's financial planning so that the pastor can attend conferences, take college courses, visit other churches, be involved in overseas mission trips and read lots of books.

Such funding does cost a church but is an investment in expanded creativity, deepened sensitivity and a rekindled passion for ministry in contemporary settings. Continual professional development and upgrading of skills help pastors do their work better, give them an increased sense of achievement and help them feel up-to-date in various expressions of ministry. Everybody in the church wins when a pastor enjoys personal fulfillment and professional development.

Here are more self-test questions regarding pastoral development lay leaders can ask themselves:

- When was the last time your church made it possible for your pastor to attend a clergy conference?
- Has your pastor ever thought about pursuing a higher level of education? Has your leadership team encouraged the pastor and offered funds to do so?
- If your church has a professional staff, are they strongly encouraged to attend at least one annual event for professional growth?
- Have you encouraged your clergy couple to attend a marriage enrichment event at least once every two years?

Consider this comparison: Would you want a physician who did not stay current regarding the latest medical advances or newest medications? Would you want a tax consultant who was unaware of the latest tax laws? Would you want your children's teachers to give up their in-service training, an obvious benefit to your child as well as to the teachers? Why not think the same way about ministers as you do other professionals?

Our culture is in a confusing time of change. Habits of church people are changing radically. Therefore, the church must refine its way of doing business in order to reach more contemporary people. No pastor can do that without encouragement and funding to continually update his skills and stir his creativity.

V. THE RIGHT OF FRIENDSHIP

To be a well-adjusted human being, everyone needs friends. But have you thought about who your pastor's best friend might be? Is it his spouse? Is it you? Is it another pastor? Is it a person in the community? In all probability, it is none of the above.

The average pastor has few genuinely close friends. Eight out of 10 pastors say they have no one besides their spouse to openly interact with about professional and personal concerns. For the majority of pastors, their closest friend is their spouse, but burdening one's mate with too many ministry details can overload emotional circuits in the marriage.

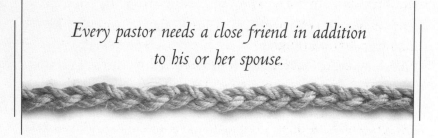

Every pastor needs a close friend in addition to his or her spouse.

Every pastor needs a close friend in addition to his or her spouse. But a serious problem exists: Many ministerial training programs, our tight-lipped culture and petty rivalries in congregations argue against it. Many seminary professors and highly placed church leaders have warned pastors not to have close friends inside or outside the church. Older colleagues often advise, "Don't trust anyone." Church members sometimes pout if they know their pastor has a close friend in the congregation. The same folks feel threatened if their pastor has friends in the community. Followed to a logical conclusion, all this means pastors are expected to be friendless.

This no-special-friendship idea is wrong and damages a pastor's wholeness. Friends are good for health and refreshing to the spirit. Without them, ministry loses much of its radiance and meaning. In a 1983 commencement address at Cornell University, Frank H. T. Rhodes offered a profound insight about friends that provides an important message to clergy: "Without friendship and the openness and trust that go with it, skills are barren and knowledge may become an unguided missile."[5] Most of us could easily identify pastors who fit that description perfectly.

So for everyone's benefit, encourage your pastor to find a best friend, a confidant. This is a favor you do your church as well as your minister. The success of her ministry likely depends on it.

I (H. B.) received a letter from a pastor's wife who tried to surprise her husband with a birthday party. She had invited several friends from the church, a few people from the community and an assortment of relatives. The party was fun. The pastor had been having tough times in his work, so it was good to see him laugh. The pastor's wife was uplifted when the party was over, but she was unprepared for what followed. The next Sunday she and her husband were confronted by several lay leaders who told them in no uncertain terms that "private parties" such as she had held for her husband were forbidden. They also reminded her that her husband was pastor of the whole church, so she could either invite everyone or stop having parties. The pastor's wife was understandably devastated and angry. No minister should be expected to forego personal friendship just because he is a pastor.

The friendships provide obvious benefits like relaxation, laughter and the opportunity to share when burdens get heavy. A friend's help often makes the difference between coping and burning out. Without friends, a pastor can be suffocated by the loneliness of ministry. Encourage your pastor to have friends inside and outside the church. A pastor, like every other human being, can do her work well *and* have close friends who are not connected to her profession in any way.

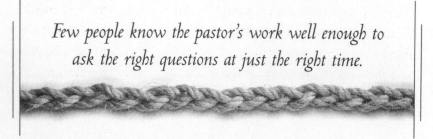

Few people know the pastor's work well enough to ask the right questions at just the right time.

Another advantage of having friends is accountability. Every pastor needs someone to ask hard questions about his marriage, walk with God, ethical and moral standards, parenting and commitments to ministry. Friends help keep a pastor principled and authentic.

Few people know the pastor's work well enough to ask the right questions at just the right time. Therefore, when your pastor finds someone who is a genuine friend, do not make her feel guilty about the association. Rather, encourage and rejoice about the richness such an association brings to his ministry. An accountability friend will help your pastor serve better and have a closer relationship with God and family.

Use the following questions to evaluate your pastor's freedom to cultivate close friendships:

- Are you a potential best friend to your pastor?
- Do you defend your pastor's right to have friends?

- How would your church handle the birthday party mentioned earlier? How would you react if you were not invited to the party?
- How can you encourage your pastor to have a friend who will hold him accountable?

VI. THE RIGHT FOR PROTECTION FROM UNREALISTIC SCRUTINY

Nearly everyone realizes how difficult it is to overlook misdirected words or insensitive acts that hurt one's mate or family. But because ministers live in glass houses, it is easy for a layperson to see a weakness in a spiritual leader. To complicate matters, people love to discuss public persons and their families; that explains the attraction of television programs like "Lifestyles of the Rich and Famous." Taking these factors into consideration, laity should not be surprised when they find their pastor is superprotective of his family. Many ministers find it difficult to tolerate even a hint of criticism against their family.

To keep this scrutiny problem in balance, several suggestions might be worth discussing in your decision-making group.

Never consider a pastor's spouse to be an unpaid assistant. Unless a "package" employment agreement was made at the interview stage, a church should not expect a minister's mate to be an unpaid assistant. In reality, the pastor's spouse is a layperson married to a minister. In the years of your pastor's service to your church, the spouse's involvement will likely increase or decrease depending on family needs, outside workload and health. Try to view the mate's involvement just as you would that of any other volunteer.

Let kids be kids. It is unfair to expect the minister's children to be role models for children in the congregation. And even if you expect it, you will not get it. At nearly every pastors' conference, several ministry couples share the pain they feel because of their children. Much of this distress is rooted in unrealistic expectations of the minister's children, either by the parents or the congregation. A play center for children in Colorado Springs has an imaginative ad that expresses this idea: "A place where kids can be kids." Why not make your church a place where kids can be kids?

Pastors' children, like all children, come into the world human and subject to the same temptations others experience. Allow a minister's children to develop normally. Talk to them like you would any child. Let them know they are loved for themselves and not because of who their parents are. Give them the benefit of the doubt, like you would your own children. Help create a climate in your church where all children and teens find it easy to seek the Savior.

Some of the saddest people in the whole world are the grown children of ministers; these children never had the opportunity to develop their own faith and uniqueness. For a lifetime, they have sought the elusive carrot of emotional and spiritual health without finding it. On the contrary, some of the most well-adjusted people of faith are those who were loved into wholeness by congregations their pastor-parent served during their childhood and adolescence.

As a lay leader, you can help encourage the spiritual and emotional development of a pastor's children. Try loving your minister's children into joyous faith. Since they are often far away from uncles and aunts and grandparents, become their extended family. Give them space to develop their identity. Allowing these children to see Christ in you may be the most important ministry you will ever accomplish. As years pass, you will see the pastor's children prosper in their spiritual development and know you had a significant part in it. That's satisfying to you and pleasing to God.

Don't ask members of the pastor's family to deliver second-hand messages. If you have something to say, say it directly to the pastor. Do not expect the spouse or children to deliver messages. Speak to the pastor yourself so the message will be clear and you will not injure the person you expect to deliver your message. No one has the right to cause a child to ask, "Dad, how come Mr. Smith is angry with you?" Or, "Mom, why are the ladies all talking about your new dress?" Or, "Dad, parents of my church friends don't think you work enough. Why would they say something like that?" Good question—why would they say that?

Christian brothers and sisters must nobly live above such foolishness. The potential damage to a child is too great for anyone to take part in such irrationality. If you want to sour children on the church or undermine their confidence in the family of God, just carelessly criticize their parents. Who wants responsibility for creating such difficult problems? Instead of tearing down your pastor in front of his family or yours, build him up. Pastors' kids beam with pride when you brag to them about their parents.

Try to answer these questions:

- When was the last time you let your minister's children know they were cherished?
- Do you praise the minister's children?
- When your pastor's kids act like kids, what do you say to their parents?
- Do you pray for your pastor's children?

VII. THE RIGHT TO FAIL

Jesus was the only perfect person in human history. He never failed. He never sinned. His character always radiated love and goodness. He is our pattern and example. Our Lord was the only one who ever walked on water, though a few of His followers have tried without success.

Pastors are never perfect imitators of their Lord. Do not expect them to be, and you will not be disappointed. Pastors do not intentionally fail, and no minister purposely wants to disillusion you or hinder the church. The nature of ministry is to give one's life to helping others find joy in living out the Christian life. Consequently, your pastor never wants to preach a poorly prepared sermon or give wrong counsel. If pastors had their way, they would never miss an appointment or make a bad decision. And if they could, they would walk on water for you. But they cannot. Regrettably, they sometimes fail.

In a congregation of senior citizens, Baby Boomers, Busters, power brokers and adolescents, no human being can keep everyone satisfied all the time. Consequently, pastors must do their best and congregations must accept their best as being good enough. Unfortunately, the best is not good enough for some church members. Those who study forced pastoral terminations believe such actions are frequently due to the unwillingness of seven or fewer people to reconcile a difference.

Can you believe it? Seven or fewer unforgiving people are allowed by the majority to force a pastor's termination. Even though Jesus taught forgiveness throughout Scripture, a small group of unforgiving church persons can determine a pastor's future and create a perilous crisis in the congregation.

There is a better way. Try following the counsel of Jesus in Matthew 18:15: "If your brother sins against you, go and show him his fault, just between the two of you. If he listens to you, you have won your brother over."

Lest anyone think we are trying to defend incompetence or laziness, let's make it clear—we do not think pastors are perfect. Nor do we believe all pastors are sincerely authentic. Some are ill-prepared for their assignment, and some would be better off in secular work. Yet it is dangerously unfair for a small group to determine the future ministry of a pastor. Surely the guidance of God must be sought. To harm those whom God has called to the ministry and anointed for service is a serious deed that produces consequences that will thunder into the future of a church. Whatever the cause of a pastor's termination, for years to come painful consequences will ricochet in every direction.

I (H. B.) once blew it big time in a church I served. No one could have felt worse about my failure than I did. My error was serious enough that it could have undermined the faith of the family I had wronged. They could have made life miserable for me throughout the congregation. I dreaded the confrontation, but it had to come. I sat defenseless in front of a brokenhearted family and asked them to forgive me. They forgave me and treated me as God treats everyone, as though I had done no wrong. As a result, I became a better pastor, and God was glorified by forgiveness given and forgiveness received.

Could that happen every time there is a misunderstanding between minister and parishioner? Probably not. Should an attempt be made to resolve every conflict? Every time. Because that is what God expects. He wants His people to pursue the spiritual development forgiveness causes in everyone involved.

Though not known as a person of faith, Theodore Roosevelt believed in the right to fail and start again. He loved to say:

It is not the critic who counts, nor the man who points out how the strong man stumbled or where the doer of deeds could have done better. The credit belongs to the man who is actually in the arena, whose face is marred by the dust and sweat and blood; who strives valiantly; who errs and comes up short again and again; who knows the great enthusiasms, the great devotions and spends himself in a worthy cause; who, at the best, knows in the end the triumph of high achievement; and who at the worst, if he fails, at least fails while daring greatly, so that his place shall never be with those cold and timid souls who know neither victory nor defeat.[6]

What an encouragement these words are to every pastor who has tried and failed. It is time to try again, and it's time for lay leaders to give their pastor another opportunity for effective ministry.

VIII. THE RIGHT OF PASSAGE

From several studies and continuing dialogue with ministers, we conclude that as many as one in four pastors has experienced at least one forced termination in the years of his service.

How does that happen? Depending on the church's governing board, a congregation can vote "no confidence" or a decision-making group can vote to terminate the pastoral relationship. Another more common, though unofficial, way is for a disgruntled group to work cunningly against the pastor, making it so difficult for her to do effective ministry that the minister chooses to leave. Another devilish technique is to start false rumors that have no basis in fact. Sadly, when such undercurrents start, there is almost no way to stop them and in time the pastor's ministry is damaged beyond repair. Ministry usually ends when credibility is destroyed.

A pastor friend suffered through six years of contention in his congregation. The church grew. People's lives were transformed. A new church building was erected. An overwhelmingly positive congregational vote gave our friend and his family the right to stay, but they finally gave up and moved.

Like a dripping faucet in the background of church life came damaging accusations and mixed messages from a small group of disgruntled people. Finally, the pastor and his family could no longer tolerate the opposition either emotionally or spiritually, so they left. The pastor's future ministry had been damaged, and the potential of the church had been sabotaged by the selfish aims of a few who simply wore the pastor down.

Such a tragedy is not right. It should not happen. But it is happening somewhere right now, even as you read these words.

Consider the dreadful fallout of forced terminations. In the process, a church is usually held hostage by people who seize control. Potential converts think that the church is a counterfeit absurdity. Disgruntled folks, when they try to pray, know who caused the havoc and who bears responsibility in God's judgment. Ministers' families are spiritually scarred forever. Even neighboring pastors feel stifled by what happens to colleagues, so morale plummets in their churches. As a result, the voice of the prophet is stilled and the challenging demands of the gospel are neglected in places well beyond the local congregation. Some ministers quit permanently; others develop a lifelong distrust of church members. Predictably, the church gets a bad name in the community, so the authenticity of the gospel is doubted in a community for years to come. The final blow comes when solid members get tired of the sham and move on to another church, leaving the congregation in control of those who provoked the problem. When this sabotage is complete, the congregation finds another pastor. Then the process starts over again, because the controllers have outwitted and outlasted the spiritually sound folks.

So the tragedy continues. Some churches are on their third or fourth round of such destructive foolishness. Busy spending big dollars on candidating and moving in a new pastor, members of dysfunctional congregations know they will face the same difficulties again in a few months or years, because nothing has changed except a former pastor has been driven out.

It is time to ask some serious questions and take drastic action. Healing prescriptions or painful surgeries are needed. Someone must champion intercession and revival.

Of course, the reverse side, long pastorates, also must be considered. Ministers should not stay forever. Churches sometimes outgrow pastors, and pastors sometimes outgrow churches. That's life. If a transition seems to be the will of God, then let it be done with grace and magnanimity.

A line from Kenny Rogers's earthy country song "The Gambler" highlights a more spiritual lesson: "You have to know when to hold them and know when to fold them." Still, there is far too much transition in every area of church life, including the moving of pastors and the migration of church members. Moving, as bad as it is, seems better than facing and solving issues that divide us. Kingdom efforts are often weakened because we are quick-change artists. There is a time to move and a time to stay the course. In many settings, more spiritually minded lay leaders are desperately needed—leaders who count the high costs of changing pastors and determine that improving an existing pastoral relationship may be much better than establishing a new one.

IX. THE RIGHT TO ORGANIZATIONAL SUPPORT

The value and difficulties of denominations and associations of churches have been debated during most of this century and will likely be debated well into the next century. We have no intention of fueling more controversy on these well-discussed issues. It appears that churches and pastors serve in denominational organizations to provide stability and direction for doctrinal issues, church colleges, efficiency and continuity of missionary ministries, church planting and care of the clergy. These issues are of obvious importance in both denominational and independent churches.

But clergy in crisis has become an urgent new dilemma facing all churches. This issue is bearing down on contemporary churches like a 32-wheeler speeding out of control down a mountain pass. This crisis has shown up in staggering proportions in all church groups, from Pentecostal to Catholic and every group in between. What was formerly ignored for so long is finally being faced. What was denied did not go away. Issues many people chose to overlook are now pushing the Church to act. Since these changes are taking place so quickly, denominational agencies are shocked and experiencing great difficulty in determining how to prioritize redemptive responses to the problem.

The Lord's army must have its troops in the best spiritual, physical and emotional fighting condition possible.

This crisis must be solved if the church is to have a viable future in many places. A church cannot be the church God wants without pastors who are holy and whole. The trashing of clergy by systems, power brokers or even pastors cannot go on much longer without the Church's passing a point of no return. No army can fight with overstressed, hungry, depressed, crippled soldiers. No army can expect to win a war when its warriors are under attack from the front by the enemy and from the rear by its own troops. No army can fight when army headquarters puts more resources into foreign aid than into defense. Yet that is exactly what the army of the Lord does in many places.

The Lord's army must have its troops in the best spiritual, physical and emotional fighting condition possible. Anything less means more soldiers will be wounded or killed in the line of fire. It also means more casualties, more deserters, more wounded, more morale problems and more people who deserve Purple Hearts.

To stimulate a more effective response to these problems, consider the following concerns and suggestions of how a denomination or association of churches can support pastors and local churches. Meanwhile, let's face the reality that these groups are made up of individuals like us, so we may need to take the first steps in response strategies. Thus, these suggestions are as much for us to implement as for anyone else.

1. Affirmation

Affirm a minister's importance as a member of the pastoral team. The attitude should be "How can our association of churches or our denomination enable the called, anointed servant of the church to do frontline ministry?"

2. Safety

Provide a safe haven for those going through emotional, relational, spiritual or physical challenges. This should be done for the sake of the pastor and his family and to insure future usefulness to the cause of Christ. Someone has to nurse the wounded back to vibrant health.

3. Pastoral Care

Develop a pastor for pastors. This person should have no administrative or credentialing authority over ministers. However caring ecclesiastical leaders may be, it is difficult for a pastor to discuss personal issues with one who has authority over her future placement.

4. Team Building
To nourish a sense of belonging, seek regular input from pastors about programs, methods and expenditures of the larger body.

5. Development
Provide annual, quality, relevant personal and spiritual development opportunities for pastors. Encourage larger churches to give scholarships to ministers serving churches with limited financial resources.

6. Benefits
Establish a plan of minimum compensation and insurance benefits for pastoral families. Such benefits could be classified as full support or bivocational. No church should expect to have a full-time pastor when it does not pay a minimum full-time salary. Neither should a pastor with small pastoral responsibilities serving in a bivocational role expect full-time support.

7. Acceptance
Encourage innovation and creativity in ministry so that all sectors of society can be reached with the gospel.

8. Fair Hearing
Provide a system of due process and interim compensation for pastors whom churches have abused. Pastors are too often cast aside at the will of a few malcontents and then viewed as suspect for the remainder of their ministry. Congregations who mistreat a pastor should be censored by the larger Church body and held financially liable until the wronged pastor can be reassigned. On the contrary, a plan is also needed to be sure a pastor is faithful

in doing ministry—no slothful servants should be tolerated in the Savior's service.

9. Spiritual Health

Promote the spiritual well-being of congregations rather than emphasizing numerical size alone. The work of all God's called servants must be seen as valuable regardless of the size of church they serve.

10. Alongside Strength

Have all ecclesiastical leaders spend a minimum of two weeks each year ministering in a local church with an average attendance of fewer than 100. Let them experience firsthand the pressures and possibilities that pastors continually face. In such a one-on-one relationship, every pastor would get to see the heart of his leaders and every official would feel the pulse of a local congregation.

X. THE RIGHT TO SPEAK OUT AGAINST SIN AND INJUSTICE

Pastors must be given the right to speak out on issues threatening the moral fiber of the nation, the church and the family. There are times in every local church and every society, like in Elijah's day, when someone must stand before the king to confront evil and speak forthrightly about the consequences of sin. Our world continues to decay morally, at least in part, because of the soft, timid words of the church concerning our local and national sins.

If pastors do not denounce sin, who will? Something must be done to stop the cancers of violence, immorality, brokenness and greed. Pastors see the firsthand consequences of sin when they show up in the lives of individuals and families. Ministers often face the gaping wounds resulting from alcohol, pornography, domestic violence, immorality and selfishness. Yet little is said and less is done to heal those wounds.

In this century, society has moved from Puritanism to hedonism. An "anything goes" stance or outright silence in the church allows immorality to flourish. It's time to confront a depraved culture that kills the unborn, accepts perversions as alternative lifestyles and tolerates violence at home and in the streets. It's time to speak. It's time to shout. It's time to yell "fire!"

> *Every pastor needs to be encouraged to speak a flaming word from God against national and individual sins in our culture.*

Every pastor needs to be encouraged to speak a flaming word from God against national and individual sins in our culture. Let's take direction from the former Anglican Bishop of Southwark: "My diocese is said to be on the boil. If that is so, I accept it as a compliment. Boiling water is better than tepid. It can cleanse and generate power."[7]

God loathes sin in churches as much as He does in society. Thus, ministers must speak out against sin in their congregations, even though some churches have lower standards for members than the local Kiwanis Club. One church in Appalachia, in order to receive reduced postage, wrote on all its mail "non-prophet organization." But that's not the way God intends a church to be. Our Father wants His church pure and clean and exemplar so He can work through it without giving Himself a bad reputation. And He wants prophets to denounce sin.

Let one fact be clearly understood—God refuses to bless a church that accommodates wickedness at any level of leadership. Unfortunately, many churches have so watered down the message of righteousness that our Lord sees us as no better than the den of thieves He so angrily rebuked (see John 2:13-16).

Every fair-minded person must encourage his pastor to speak the truth in love as a Christ-exalting corrective. The list of sins inside the church is long, frightening and even nauseating. Gossip, backbiting, slander, malice, immorality, spouse-swapping, financial scams, overindulgence and subtle worldliness in a thousand forms make the church too weak to fight and too guilty to seek God's face.

Many churches want only comforting words from their minister. But any congregation that keeps her pastor silent about sin will soon become as corrupt as the world. And any pastor who refuses to call people to repentance is guilty of malfeasance. Words of truth from Holy Scripture must be wholeheartedly supported. From the start of a pastor's ministry in a new church setting, he must be given liberty to denounce sin and preach righteousness. Empower your pastor to speak redemptively against sin in society; encourage him to stand for righteousness; and support his efforts to expose darkness with the white light of God.

LET'S MAKE A DIFFERENCE

This chapter has not been easy to write. It is filled with tender compassion and tough love for the church because we care. We want the Church of Jesus Christ renewed in our time. The essential message we have written seems demanding and radical, and some readers may think, controversial. Some of what we have said leaves opportunity for misunderstanding or even objection. But try to hear our heart cry—too many pastors are forced to suffer for doing the right thing. Too many congregations are being sabotaged by shallow leaders who want control more than they want Christ and want power more than they want The Power.

Without spiritually committed, courageous pastors, the contemporary church will steadily decline and society will become more corrupt. Pastors are not the only persons needed for this war, but it cannot be won without them. When pastors are in jeopardy, the church could lose the war. We are in a battle for the soul of the church and the eternal destiny of the lost. Winning will not be easy, but it is possible.

For too long the church has played into the enemy's hands by trashing pastors and by speaking too softly about what sin does in our lives, families and society. We beg you to carefully consider what we have written. Weigh it conscientiously. Discuss it. Talk it over with your decision-making group. Ask your pastor to share his heart on these issues, perhaps for the first time. Pray about it. Then, do something to spiritually revolutionize the environment of your church.

It is time for lay leaders in the church to lock arms and join hearts with pastors. Let's move as one. Let's keep ourselves pure and holy so that the Father will not be embarrassed to keep company with us. Let's ask the Author and Finisher of our faith to enable us. He will. Our Lord wants pastors and parishioners to move in a mighty, unified effort to change the world and revive the church.

Try in every feasible way to renew the spirit and stimulate your pastor's courage. Here is a short list on how to start:

- Love your pastor into greatness.
- Believe in him as a holy person.

- Apply her preaching to your life.
- Release him from repetitive routines.
- Make the logistics of her living as easy as possible.
- Do not waste his sacrifice.
- Encourage her to dream big dreams.
- Treat him as generously as you treat your boss.
- Start an affirmation campaign about your pastor today.
- Try to see your church through the eyes of the Savior.
- Commit to be a holy person who pleases God in all things.

Renewal Strategies for Lay Leaders: How to Liberate Your Pastor to Greatness

1. Encourage your pastor to dream big.
2. Assure your pastor of your prayer support.
3. Promote adequate salary and regular raises for your minister.
4. Encourage your pastor's professional growth.
5. Champion your minister's need to have friends.
6. Shelter your pastor and family from unfair scrutiny.
7. Allow your pastor the right to fail.
8. Provide your pastor the right of passage when needed.
9. Support your minister's right to organizational support.
10. Champion your leader's right to speak out against sin and injustice.

Notes

1. Louis E. Boone, *Quotable Business* (New York: Random House, 1992), p. 200.
2. *Bathroom Book*, vol. 1 (Salt Lake City, UT: Compact Classics, 1992), pp. 3-4.
3. Norman Vincent Peale, *The Power of Positive Thinking* (New York: Ballantine Books, 1996), n.p.
4. James B. Simpson, *Simpson's Contemporary Quotes* (New York: Houghton Mifflin, 1988), p. 65.
5. Ibid., p. 239.
6. Theodore Roosevelt (paper presented at the Sorbonne, April 23, 1910), n.p.
7. Robert K. Hudnut, *Surprised by God* (New York: Association Press, 1967), p. 68.

Appreciate your pastoral leaders who gave you the Word of God. Take a good look at the way they live, and let their faithfulness instruct you, as well as their truthfulness.

HEBREWS 13:7, *THE MESSAGE*

CHAPTER 10

49 WAYS TO LOVE YOUR PASTOR

HOW TO USE THE BIG THREE "A" WORDS

Lord of our church,
Thank You for the ministry family who serves our
church.
We praise You for their insights,
their faith,
their sacrifices,
their training,
their devotion,
their faithfulness.
Teach us a thousand new ways to show our love.
We cherish them for their work's sake.
Amen.

Businesses, large and small, are discovering how much CEOs, vice presidents, janitors and all workers in between need the big three A words: "Affirmation," "Appreciation" and "Admiration." Every human being needs a generous proportion of all three. And these expressions of affection are especially needed for and from persons with whom we work, live and serve, particularly pastors.

Interesting results take place when the three *A* words are sincerely expressed in business environments. More quality work gets done. Employees enjoy their jobs more, fewer mistakes are made, and workers move less often to other jobs. Personnel problems grow fewer in number and absenteeism declines. Caring businesses have more customers and sell more products. Maybe the business world has discovered something they can teach the church.

The big three *A* words—"Affirmation," "Appreciation" and "Admiration"—also work wonderfully well in marriages and families. One blustery, take-charge-type father claimed he never needed admiration or thanks, but he melted when his three-year-old daughter said, "You are the best daddy in the whole world." That same tough guy feels so special when he affirms his wife as mother, wife and best friend. And he goes off to his job in the morning singing when his wife says, "You are the best husband any woman could ever have."

USING THE BIG THREE *A* WORDS AT CHURCH

Affirmation, appreciation and admiration all work well and are greatly needed in the church. In many congregational settings, insightful lay church leaders wish a three-*A*-words climate existed or could be cultivated, but they don't know how to start. Others don't miss it, because they have never experienced it, but they will like if they ever do. Though many people realize how important the three *A* words are, for some strange reason we find it hard to build strong acceptance and love in our church relationships, especially in communication between spiritual leaders and lay leaders.

The ability to cherish is in short supply in too many congregations. Without considering strengths, we tend to overemphasize shortcomings. We are often quick to judge and slow to praise. Too often the 1 percent rule controls. This rule focuses on 1 percent of what is wrong and misses the 99 percent that is right. For example, perfect attendance for 50 Sundays is often overlooked when a person misses two services. One sentence in a sermon gets belittled without considering the good said before and after the troubling part. Having a bad teaching day, a Sunday School teacher may be criticized for a poorly presented lesson while many years of devoted, effective service are ignored.

All these situations can be bettered with the three *A* words. A grand place to begin this effort in your church would be to go out of your way to show your pastor that she is cherished. With imagination and effort, you can set in motion many ways to build a cherishing environment for your spiritual leader. Think of the agreeable results. Likely she will relish ministry more, be more effective and stay longer in a pastoral assignment. In return, you and your church will enjoy working with a fulfilled servant of God. Then, your church atmosphere will radiate love and wholeness as suspicion, criticism and adversarial relationships are minimized or forgotten.

Could it be that the Head of the Church is promising lay leaders "If you will befriend My servant and give special attention to his personal and family needs, I will bless your church in ways you never imagined and you will enjoy your efforts in My church more"?

Before specific strategies for expressing appreciation, affirmation and admiration are discussed, these principles need to be considered:

1. Authentic

Affirmation should be positive and true without a hint of what

someone called "negative/positive." One lay leader who intended to honor his pastor said, "Even though some have had problems with our pastor, I love him dearly." That comment is veiled
hostility, which does no good.

2. Unrehearsed

Spontaneous affirmation carries more weight than planned
speeches. Of course, both spontaneous and planned affirmations are needed. But this principle simply nudges every
Christian leader to cultivate a spirit of gratitude and generosity
so that affirming others becomes natural or even instinctive.

3. Genuine

Affirmation means more when it comes from a friend or from
someone who wants to be our friend. The power of kindness is
stronger when it comes from those with whom we have the closest relationships. Those who know the pastor best and work
closest with her should express their appreciation and affirmation first and most frequently.

Do something. An act of kindness carries more weight than
a thousand words. Since it is our nature as Christians to want to
serve, this principle should be easy for us to believe and achieve.

Everyone needs praise. Even those who deny their need of
affirmation need it. One old saint was praising her pastor for his
faithfulness to the shut-ins. He embarrassingly replied, "I'm just
doing what I want to do. Besides, it's my duty. Please don't praise
me for doing my duty." After a few moments of thought, the old
saint replied, "Pastor, if you don't need affirmation, why do you
seem to enjoy it so much?" Even the most capable, apparently
self-sufficient leader never outgrows the need for affirmation
and appreciation.

Affirmation, appreciation and admiration are like a
boomerang—it comes back around and helps the person who

gives affirmation fully as much as it helps the one who receives it. In some strange way, giving affirmation makes one feel more fulfilled as a person. But we are often too busy, too preoccupied or too stressed out to realize that the recognition we give enriches our lives too.

4. Good Gossip

Positive secondhand affirmation will be reported on a church gossip line nearly as quickly as a negative report. It's fun to say something affirming about a pastor to a layperson and then wait to see how long it takes for him to tell the pastor. It usually happens pretty quickly. In the process, the initiator, the receiver and the reporter are all encouraged. Management consultant Janis Mien says, "When someone says something good about another person and I tell that person about it, she seems to get more reinforcement value from it than if she had received the compliment firsthand."[1]

5. Attractive Magnetism

Appreciation for your pastor often attracts others to your church. They are more easily drawn to a congregation that speaks glowing, kind comments about its pastor. Speaking affirmatively about your pastor is an inexpensive advertisement for your local church and for the cause of Christ.

6. Love That Multiplies

Many contemporary churches need a revival of love. They need to love Christ more, love each other more, love the world more and love to their leaders more. A good place to start is to put new emphasis on loving your pastor as he serves Christ and you. Love is contagious. Many congregations find they increase love in the church as a whole by starting with their pastor and family. The pastor in turn starts loving the congregation more. Members of the congregation follow these leads, and, before long, the church becomes a fellowship of love and acceptance.

7. Match Affirmation to the Individual
Give gifts of appreciation with the individual's preferences, values and tastes in mind. A golf putter, even an expensive one, will not make much difference to one who does not play golf.

8. Make a Memory
The three *A* words work best when the recognition creates a story or memory the pastor can tell his family, fellow pastors and young ministers for years to come. More creative readers of this chapter might ask their pastor to point out strategies in this chapter that would inspire him.

9. Match Affirmations and Achievements
Ten years of pastoral service deserve a different depth of affirmation than one year's service. Three years of heavy responsibility in developing a church plant or four years in a church building/relocation project are examples of activities that stand worthy of generous recognition.

10. Err on the Side of Generosity
Too many people economize in their affirmations and gift giving. When selecting a gift, look for quality rather than the lowest possible price. A quality necktie might be more treasured than an inexpensive shirt.

11. Start Now
Follow your heart and express it now. Do not allow good intentions to fade before turning them into deeds of love and kindness. Expressing the three *A* words is a good practice for the

decision-making group in your church, but it can also be done spontaneously and joyously by individuals.

THE 49 WAYS

Even if you have been your pastor's thorn in the flesh for years, you can change. Even if you have been one who draws stamina and strength from a pastor but never returns anything, you can start providing emotional and spiritual support for your pastor. Even if you think of your pastor as a rock of spiritual strength who needs nothing from anyone else, you can become an affirmer of your minister. Even if you are a veteran grumbler who expects pastors to be better, nobler and holier than you, you can change. Even if you have never thought to encourage your pastor, you can start now.

If you fall into any of these categories, or others we have not mentioned, you can turn good intentions to loving deeds by using some of these 49 ways to express affirmation and appreciation to one of the most influential people in your life.

1. Speak up
Say something wonderful to affirm your pastor. Affirm her competence and commitment to your church. Mention the sermon when you greet the minister at the door following a service and say "Thank you for so many new thoughts and for the passion with which you preached them."

2. Write it down
A short, handwritten, first-class note that arrives on the pastor's desk by Tuesday or Wednesday is a thoughtful way to keep your pastor aware of what his Sunday ministry is doing for you. Or simply write a note following a demanding funeral, saying, "The Lord really helped you with a tough assignment. I'm glad you are

such a sensitive pastor. I am proud of you." It always means more when people take time to write their affirmations, even those they have already given verbally.

A creative lay leader in a Southern California church writes a word of appreciation on a copy of Sunday's bulletin and pushes it under the door of the pastor's office. One teen in North Carolina does the same thing with Sunday's bulletin, but he puts the note under the windshield wiper of the pastor's car.

3. Appoint a spokesperson

Ask the pastor to allow a member of the congregation to make an announcement during a public meeting, and use that time to praise your minister. The spokesperson should be a respected leader of the congregation. If workers in the secular marketplace rate a pat on the back as an important incentive for future efforts, then a public pat on the back will encourage your pastor as well.

4. Phone or fax the pastor

Call or fax your pastor with a word of thanks or affirmation. Fax machines and e-mail give parishioners new technology for expressing the three *A* words for their pastors.

Tell the minister, "Just wanted to tell you how much you are helping me grow spiritually." "I only called to say thanks and to let you know that you are helping me become more like Christ." If you get the answering machine, you do not have to ask for a return call; just leave a message telling your pastor you will be thinking about his positive impact on your life all week. Be as specific as possible with your words of praise. One woman prayed on the pastor's answering machine, asking God to supply all her pastor's needs and some of his wants. Power in prayer is greatly multiplied when a person hears you pray for him by name—that does not happen to pastors often.

5. Give credit for good ideas

When discussing an idea that originates with the pastor, be sure to give her credit. You can say, "I have been thinking a lot lately about an idea the pastor shared with us months ago. At that time, I was a little cold to the proposal, but I now see how important it is."

6. Name something after the pastor

One church named its new sanctuary after its pastor. Another congregation honored its pastor by naming the boardroom after him. A couple in Tennessee named their first child after their pastor—what pride she felt. A church in Maine gave a scholarship to a deserving student in the pastor's name; the idea was so well received, they established a permanent scholarship for future students from their church.

7. Improve the pastor's working environment

Nearly every pastor's office or study needs to be upgraded or expanded because of a lack of bookcases, insufficient filing cabinets, out-of-date office equipment or old, battered furniture. Most ministers will be more productive in an inviting environment.

If a faithful pastor spends the major part of her time in her study, is it too much to expect that it be comfortably furnished and cheerfully decorated? Furnish the study the way the pastor prefers rather than the way some committee decides. While many churches might not be able to afford to totally refurbish the office in a week or a month, nearly every church could do significant upgrades over a year's time. An extra filing cabinet is a small price for making a pastor feel cherished. A new desk is a modest expenditure when it makes a pastor feel good about her work and her acceptance by the congregation. Why not make your pastor's work space the nicest office in the neighborhood and the most functional room in the church? Many people, if given the idea, would donate for this purpose outside the regular budget.

One church fussed and fumed about the pastor's installing a phone in his car. The price was about $20 per month, but they lost hundreds of dollars of good will and wasted energy in the feeling of rejection the pastor experienced. Obviously, a church cannot always provide everything a pastor would like. But for reasonable expenditures, it is advisable to provide them because of the good will and satisfaction that follow. Then everyone wins. Try thinking the way the minister thinks about his workplace and give him tools to do his work effectively.

8. Celebrate birthdays and wedding anniversaries

The spouses of employees are usually not a significant and visible part of the work climate in secular professions, businesses and government jobs. The church is different. Feature and highlight your pastor's mate and family—*love them into greatness*.

One pastor asked a budding pianist, the son of an evangelist, to give a classical concert in his church. The program was a glowing success. In a few days, the evangelist faxed this note, "Anyone who loves and accepts my son is immediately loved, accepted and appreciated by me." The lesson here is for a congregation to give extraordinary care and affection to the pastor's family on special days and to celebrate their important achievements.

9. Promote Pastor Appreciation Day

Focus on the Family has led the way by issuing a national call for congregations to honor pastors each October. The reports from pastors about how they feel cherished and special are beautiful and inspiring.

Make Pastor Appreciation Day a new tradition in your church. When the idea is announced and promoted, many in your congregation will find some unique way to express affirmation for the pastor. As one teenage football player remarked, "Next to my family, Pastor Gregory is the most important person in my life. It's time we showed him how important he really is."

10. Send flowers, balloons or plants

Even though most people think flowers are exclusively for women, try sending flowers to the pastor's home, especially on Christmas and Easter or a "just because" day. A flowering plant delivered to the pastor's home in the dead of winter creates a never-to-be-forgotten memory. Remember, compensation is what your church pays your pastor for doing his job, but recognition is what you do to show affirmation, affection and appreciation.

11. Plan an Anniversary Sunday

Some churches have a tradition of celebrating their pastor's service to their church on the anniversary of his first Sunday there. Many African-American churches do this well. Someone in the leadership group needs to be given responsibility for implementing this idea.

One Florida church buys its pastor a gift certificate to the best men's store in the area so he can purchase a new suit each year. Imagine how many times during the year someone comments on his suit and how he beams with pride when he says, "My wonderful congregation bought this suit for me."

12. Go overboard at Christmas

Often Christmas is a lonely time for a pastoral family, especially after all the activities of Christmas Sunday are over at the church. Pastors may feel loneliness at Christmas, because they live too many miles from extended family to visit during the Christmas season. Meanwhile, church families are busy with their own festivities.

A special way to honor your pastor at Christmas is to write a generous amount into the church budget for a gift and then supplement that amount by asking everyone in the congregation to contribute to a special Christmas offering. When these two income sources are combined, any church can give its pastoral family generous Christmas gifts. A Scrooge-type remarked, "We pay our pastor, so we don't need to do much at Christmas." To which a generous person replied, "Our gifts have nothing to do with pay and everything to do with love."

A Florida church I (Neil) once pastored had a tradition of putting individual money gifts into Christmas cards for their pastors. One Christmas, the pastoral family received $750 in individual Christmas cards. Love makes us into givers and blesses the one who gives.

13. Honor achievements

One Colorado church had a celebration beyond all celebrations when their pastor was ordained. Many members drove many miles to attend the ceremony and then had an all-church celebration the next Sunday to honor their pastor's ordination. They took pictures of the ordination event, had the photos enlarged and displayed them in the foyer.

Another church built "a memory" when they learned their pastor had completed 30 years in ministry. This congregation in the South honored its pastor with a great banquet to which congregation and community people were invited. Videotapes were played and messages read from former parishioners. What an evening they enjoyed, celebrating the faithfulness of God as expressed through their minister's work and service.

A church being served by a wonderful student minister had a great celebration when she graduated from seminary; in fact, the celebration was so gratifying that the young pastor decided to accept the church's invitation to continue as their pastor after she graduated. The members of that congregation believe that their affirmation was really an investment in the quality of pastoral leadership they enjoy as this young pastor develops into a mature minister. They discovered that affirmation often pays more than it costs.

14. Use your creativity and imagination

One management specialist remarked about affirming business leaders, "The way we see it, spending one dollar on something unique and clever is better than spending $50 on something ordinary and forgettable."[2] Translated into the practices of a church, that means leaders should be creative and imaginative. Your originality might include the use of computer banners, spoof certificates, free lunches, coupons for baby-sitting or shoe shines, balloons, and coffee mugs with affirmative sayings on them.

15. Present plaques and certificates

Many pastors have a whole wall of certificates and plaques in their offices. You might think a pastor would not enjoy more plaques or certificates. Don't kid yourself—the more the better. Every plaque and certificate reminds a pastor of the love and affection of someone at a particular point in his pastoral pilgrimage. Make sure the plaque is well designed, appropriately framed and worthy of being hung in a place of distinction for years to come.

16. Create a Hall of Fame

Create a photo hall of fame where pictures of the present and all previous pastors are displayed. It will take a little work to secure pictures of former pastors, but it is a worthy effort and helps your present pastor feel cherished. It is a church's way of assuring their present pastor that she is as important to them as anyone who has ever served there.

17. Hide surprise Post-it Notes

Write five or more Post-it Notes and leave them in conspicuous places on your pastor's desk, in his briefcase, in the front of his Bible and in his car.

One thoughtful laywoman carries yellow notes in her purse and writes a note of thanks for Sunday and places it on the door of the pastor's study at church or on the pulpit just before the next service. Once she put a note in his pulpit Bible; she thought he preached even better that day—and he probably did.

18. Host appreciation dinners

Organize your lay leaders so that one couple hosts the pastor and spouse for an appreciation dinner once each month. Set a regular monthly date so that the pastor can schedule it several months in advance. Ask each host couple to cover the cost of the dinner. Then provide a budget from the church so that each host couple can purchase a small gift for the clergy couple, to be presented at the monthly dinner.

19. Initiate a "Did you know you are making a difference?" letter

As a surprise to your pastor, ask each member of your decision-making group to come to your next meeting with a brief statement titled, "How Our Pastor Is Making a Spiritual Difference in Our Lives." Ask those who write the statements to be as specific as possible. Because every pastor wants to make a difference, this exercise in affirmation will create a spiritual and emotional bond between your pastor and your decision-making group that you never knew could exist.

20. Give a flip-chart thank-you

About twice a year, post a flip chart near the front entrance of your church where people can list thank-yous and words of appreciation for your pastor and his family. This is especially inspiring after some big achievement in the church or after some great loss has occurred, such as a number of people moving away, because an emotional letdown often follows. Those are good times to double or triple your affirmation and apprecia- tion. The real message is "We are in this great work together, and you can count on us."

21. Provide magazine subscriptions

Magazine subscription prices have increased drastically in the last few years because of rising paper and postage costs. For this reason, most pastors cannot subscribe to as many maga- zines as they wish. Send your pastor a personal check for $25 to $50, suggesting the money be spent for new magazine sub- scriptions. Then every time the magazine comes during the year, she is prompted to feel cherished because of your thoughtfulness.

22. Surprise your pastor with random acts of kindness

A few years ago, a lay leader from Nebraska was buying gas in a northeast Colorado convenience store along the interstate. He had just come from a great Promise Keepers rally in Boulder, Colorado, led by Bill McCartney, that honored pastors. At the gas pumps, the lay leader struck up a conversation with a stranger who turned out to be a pastor. The lay leader had never met the pastor before, but when he went into the station to pay for his own gas, in a moment of inspiration, he also paid for the pastor's gas. After the layman drove away and the pas- tor tried to pay, the station attendant told him his bill ($23.45) had been paid by the man who had just left. The pastor was so surprised that he wrote H. B. at Focus on the Family to say he had never felt so cherished in all the years of his ministry— what a grand return on $23.45. That pastor, for all the remaining years of his ministry, will tell that story over and over.

Think of a way to honor your pastor right now. What random act of kindness would he appreciate most?

23. Buy something for the pastor's hobby

One pastor has a model-train collection, another has a stamp collection, another restores antique cars, another loves tennis, another works with wood, another loves golf and another has a collection of preacher figurines. For each of those hobbies, the pastor could use something he does not have. Listen carefully to what the minister says about his hobbies. Ask his spouse about what he could use. You can make a friend for life by simply buying a special tool or giving a needed accessory.

24. Secure tickets to special events

A pastor wants to take time off to attend the symphony. But she never takes time to do so, even though she could afford it and her husband wants to go. Why not buy them tickets for the best symphony concert of the season? Ask them to go with you. Make sure you arrange the time and date early enough so that your pastor can plan the time in her schedule. Her spouse will think you are the greatest!

25. Provide a book budget

Most pastors have preferences concerning the books they would like to have in order to expand their library. Many young pastors have a list of books they hope to buy in the future. If such a list exists, try to find out which one has top priority. If you cannot get this information, purchase a gift certificate for his favorite bookstore. Every time your pastor uses that book for years to come, he will remember your kindness. Just today I (Neil) used a commentary and a thesaurus given to me by friends whom I remember with gratitude.

Since books are the tools of the pastor's profession—as needed as saws, hammers and pliers for the carpenter—try to establish a book budget for your pastor. Even the more well-paid pastors are likely to need more books than they can afford. Though many churches will not be able to start with large amounts in this budget, start where you can and then increase the amount each year. Budgeting $75 to $100 per month is a good place to start.

26. Fund trips away

Though you may not be able to spend church funds for this purpose, why not ask three or four persons to help you fund two nights away at a place to be chosen by your pastoral couple? If they have young children or teenagers, arrange for the kids to stay with a church family who has children about the same ages as the pastor's children—a night out for the kids too. Be sure the couple has enough money to cover all expenses so that the trip puts no strain on a limited budget. A pastoral couple will show their appreciation for months by doing better quality work, accomplished by two rested, cherished people.

27. Share a credit card

The pastoral family is about to take a vacation, and you know they are short of money. Why not give them the use of your credit card for five fill-ups at the gas station? At $25 per fill-up, that amounts to $125.

Most of us have spent that sum for something much less important in the past and will probably do so again. For churches who provide car allowances, you might wish to give the pastor full use of those credit cards when she is on vacation—an investment in a refreshed family to do even more effective ministry during the next 12 months.

28. Push for self-care

Increasingly, our society is coming to understand that self-care of the human body and soul is one of the most important things a leader can do. Corporations sometimes buy "key executive" insurance that pays large sums of money to the company if their key leader dies. The insurance is a frank admission that the company depends greatly on certain leaders. Why not give attention to the health and spiritual well-being of your pastor by seeing to it that he takes care of himself? This means your pastor must take time away to recharge spiritual batteries, get needed exercise and have regular medical care.

Spiritual self-care can be achieved by suggesting your pastor take one day per month away at a quiet place for reading, reflection and renewal. The location could be someone's vacation home, a retreat center or even a Catholic renewal center. Catholic renewal centers offer a quiet hotel-like room for prayer, reflection and rest at a minimum cost; sometimes meals are even provided as well as the use of a devotional library. Physical renewal can be achieved by using a health club, playing sports and taking advantage of a nearby church gym. Regular medical exams should be encouraged to prevent larger health problems coming as a surprise.

29. Strategize early acceptance

When a new pastor comes to serve your church, see to it that strategies are in place so that your pastor and his family feel instantly accepted. If the new minister is qualified to be chosen as your pastor, he is worthy of full acceptance without reservations. Of course, members of your congregation may be grieving for the pastor who moved away, and some may even feel abandoned. But the new pastor is not responsible for these feelings. He desperately needs immediate acceptance to get started with ministry. Take this new family into your heart and home as soon as possible.

In the official decision-making group, design and assign specific acceptance strategies during the start-up phase. If you brainstorm about this need in your decision-making group, you will be amazed at the many ways people are eager to help.

30. Suggest books from related fields
Many books in fields outside the pastor's regular reading requirements may be useful to her. Since it is difficult for a pastor to keep up-to-date in her field of interest, she cannot be expected to know about books in other fields. Business, management, biographies and social-issue books will do much to enrich the pastor's thinking and preaching.

31. Make sure the housing arrangement is fair.
If the church owns a parsonage, be sure regular attention is given to the upkeep of the property. If the parsonage is the best-kept house on the block, it gives a great testimony for the church. Ask a new pastoral family what they would like to see changed in the parsonage. Replacing carpets, even before they are completely worn out, is a lot less expensive than moving bills for a new pastor. An outspoken church controller in a congregation in a nearby state who said, "We can't afford to replace the carpet in the parsonage," was met by a young professional woman in the decision-making group who said, "We can't afford not to!" These questions usually should be directed to the pastor's spouse, especially if she is the family nestkeeper.

If the church provides a housing allowance, be sure the dollar amount is adequate. Remember, when pastors are given the option to own their own homes, they usually stay longer.

Someone will raise the equity issue and ask, "If we give the pastor a housing allowance, the church will not gain the equity." Such a comment can be addressed with a counterquestion,

"Would you want the people you work for to own the equity in your home? If you worked for IBM, would you want the corporation to collect your equity so that when you retired, you had no funds for housing?" Fairness and generosity are the standards for deciding these issues.

32. Take a surprise gift to the pastor's home
Do a small act of kindness planned especially for the pastor and her family, like bringing them a plate of freshly baked chocolate-chip cookies, a loaf of hot bread, a fruit basket you made up, fresh melons from the country fruit stand, a jar of jelly, or a fat pumpkin at Halloween season. One layperson goes by the Christmas tree lot as soon as the trees arrive and pays in advance for the pastor's tree and then advises the minister and his family to go choose any tree they want.

33. Purchase car-wash coupons
In many cities, coupons for car washes can be purchased in advance. Of course, prices will vary according to location, but with this gift, the pastor remembers the kindness of the giver every time the car is washed.

34. Organize a LifeSaver award
One church honored its pastor by giving him two dozen packages of LifeSavers. The congregation called the presentation the LifeSaver Award, because the pastor had worked for three months without a much-needed staff member. The executive committee of the decision-making group then took the pastor and the new staff member to a fine restaurant for lunch. The pastor kept the LifeSavers on his desk and offered them to people who came to see him. Of course, he commented on their significance to everyone to whom he offered a LifeSaver. That's a lot of positive feedback for a small expression of appreciation.

The new staff member also felt cherished by this creative gesture.

35. Do something out of the ordinary

Arrange a hot-air balloon ride; provide a round of golf; rent a red sports car for the pastor to drive for a month; individualize a mug with the pastor's picture on it; print his picture on T-shirts for his family; arrange for a cruise; present a certificate for a family portrait; present a certificate for a night or two at a bed-and-breakfast; buy a newspaper ad or even a billboard ad with the pastor's picture on it that says "Our pastor is loved."

36. Purchase a desk accessory

Get an accessory that the pastor enjoys using often. Here is how this idea affected pastors we know: A desk clock given by a church committee assures one pastor he is loved. To another pastor an upscale letter opener and scissors, used several times every day, provide a happy remembrance of a Sunday School class who gave the gift. A picture frame given by church members reminds another pastor of the love of those friends and displays a picture of his family—two happy memories for the price of one. A leather desk mat reminds the pastor of a family he served during their loss of a loved one.

37. Organize a testimonial potluck

Too often testimonial dinners are left until retirement or times of resignations or departure. Why not organize a testimonial dinner every year or two where persons are asked to share specific instances in which the pastor served them? Someone from the decision-making group might express appreciation for ideas, programs and ministries the pastor made possible in your church. Because your pastor's impact on your church is so significant, she needs to be recognized from time to time in front of the entire congregation.

38. Make the pastor's family feel special

Think of creative ways you can affirm the pastor's spouse and children. List their accomplishments in the newsletter or post them on the church's bulletin board. Personally congratulate the child or spouse for their achievements. Let them know you love them and think they are special.

Sharing a parent with the church places unique demands on the children, even as it provides them with unusual privileges. Many grown children of pastors give up on the church because of some unfortunate experience during childhood. All of this could be avoided or even forgotten had the congregation intentionally showered love on the children. Whatever the age of each child, make sure they know they are cherished.

The pastor's children who live at home can be affirmed every Sunday when you see them at church—"You look wonderful"; "Your family is a great example to our church"; "Everyone thinks you are special." One grandparent couple in a church I (Neil) served gave my children a dollar bill nearly every time they met the children in church—two children multiplied by about 50 Sundays per year meant this couple gave my children about $100 a year. My sons, now grown men, still have happy memories of that couple.

Children away at college can be remembered with letters, cards, care packages and small gifts. Grown children can be invited back to the church for special events. Help the pastor's children know that you appreciate the fact that ministry is so often a family affair.

39. Brag about the pastor to his family

One innovative corporation sends a letter of praise to an employee's family at the end of a long or hard project, thanking them for their support and acknowledging the important work their family did for the company. Why not send a similar letter once or twice a year to your pastor's family?

40. Institute the Golden Rule

See to it that your pastor is treated as well by the church as you would want to be treated by your employer. Too often in the church we think of pastoral leaders as simply doing their duty and as being expendable if we disagree with their decisions. Take care to see that your pastor is treated fairly in regard to time away, vacation time, working hours, compensation and raises. In too many settings, the pastor is forced to carry the financial burden when a church faces economic downturns that have nothing to do with her. Create a climate in your decision-making group and in the congregation in which your spiritual leader will always be treated with generosity and fairness.

41. Provide a personal computer and/or copy machine

Computers and copy machines are wonderful tools for sermon preparation. Even a pastor who knows little about office technology should be encouraged to see all the ways these two tools can assist him in his preparation and research. After a little investigation and training, your pastor will forever appreciate the day he was urged to step into the computer age.

42. Put a little money where your heart is

Put $10 or $20 in a birthday card addressed to your pastor.

One couple in a Florida church paid for six months of piano lessons for the pastor's children when they learned their church-planting pastor could not afford the lessons.

A congregation whose church and parsonage were located in a radically deteriorating neighborhood with inferior schools paid the annual tuition for the pastor's children to attend a quality private school.

43. Give a food gift

One year, a pastor received three turkeys for Thanksgiving.

Imagine her joy when she gave two of them away, saying, "The generous people at our church gave us three turkeys, and we wanted to share one with you."

A variety of food gifts can be given to your pastor and her family: out-of-season fruits like strawberries in winter, fruit-of-the-month clubs, seafood, jams and jellies, a variety of nuts or candy—and the list goes on. One farmer puts meat in the pastor's freezer every fall. When someone takes you to a special place for dinner or bakes you some gourmet food, you remember it for years—so will your pastor.

44. Maintain a surprise gift box

Most of us frequently see small items that remind us of our pastor. When you see those items, simply purchase them and set them aside for your pastor until you have accumulated six or seven of them. We have a friend who travels extensively and shops valiantly; she keeps a box she calls her "Neil and Bonnie" box and fills it each year with things she knows we would love.

Examples of gifts you might consider are small books, Christmas-tree ornaments, stationery, date books, calendars, pictures, key chains, note pads with appropriate sayings, candlesticks, bookends, mugs, picture frames, CDs, pocket flashlights, golf balls, tire gauges, small office supplies or even a Swiss army knife.

45. Develop encouragement events

Statistics indicate that pastors most often decide to move or resign when they are discouraged about their ministry. This often happens when the church finances are tight, attendance is low, some crisis overtakes the church, or a key person moves or dies. Then too there are those many private issues that burden a pastor—issues a pastor cannot discuss with church members.

Since the effect of these events on a pastor is usually reflected in his mood, lay leaders will know exactly when to plan an encouragement activity for the pastor. It can be a part of a regular monthly board meeting, a midweek service or a planned bombardment of encouragement cards from people the pastor has helped in the last few months. One church leader in a midwestern state arranged for five different persons to call the pastor with words of encouragement each day for a week; think how well that pastor must have preached the next Sunday. Later the minister joked that the program saved the church from having to find a new pastor. Though he appeared to be joking, he was right on target. Pastors, like most other people, find it difficult to be effective, innovative and spiritually alert when they feel discouraged, uncherished and unappreciated.

46. Offer to help

One youthful early retiree volunteers every Monday morning to perform any task at the church, run any errand or visit anyone the pastor suggests. On Sunday afternoon or evening, he contacts the pastor to find out what his assignments are for the next day. He never resists what the pastor asks him to do—they both understand that his Monday mission is to help the pastor follow up on anything that is left over from Sunday. He even insists that he can save the minister time by doing personal errands for the pastor, like making a trip to the post office, bank, hardware store, shoe repair shop, cleaners or car wash.

47. Make dreams come true

Listen closely to the dream list of your pastor and his family. Some of their dreams can easily be accomplished with a small budget and a little imagination. Perhaps your pastor's family dreams about mountain hikes, a trip to Disney World, water skiing or two days at the beach. Appoint a member of the congregation to be in charge of scouting for clues and then surprise your pastor by making his doable dreams come true.

48. Provide conference funding

Some of the most important new ideas for contemporary ministry are launched and explained at conferences. Ask your pastor which conferences she would like to attend. If she acts as if attendance would be impossible, find out the reason. The problem often stems from lack of funds, so she is slow to tell anyone about the need.

49. Arrange foreign mission and/or Holy Land travel

Travel outside the United States is getting more and more common for ministers. Hundreds of pastors testify that their ministry has been changed forever by giving a week of service to a mission ministry outside the United States. Others will tell you that the Bible came alive in their preaching when they visited the Holy Land. Regrettably, these trips are usually thought to be impossible when a pastor has a young family or when he serves a smaller church. Instead of thinking it is financially out of the question, someone in your church should take the lead to see if it is possible. Often church members would be willing to give to finance such a trip if they realized its significance and feasibility. Instead of talking about how impossible it sounds, check out the prices and ask about the programs. You may find that it is less expensive than you first thought. Such a trip will create an enriching memory for your pastor that he will never forget—and your congregation will reap the spiritual benefits.

TIME TO BEGIN

Lest we get mired in the details of how to show a pastor and family that they are loved, let's go back to the three *A* words—"Appreciation," "Affirmation" and "Admiration." For a pastor to stay the course, to fight the good fight and be spiritually strong, it is absolutely necessary that he know that the majority of the congregation is grateful for the impact of his ministry.

Several of these ideas for showing your love can be implemented immediately. Others can be initiated at the next meeting of the decision-making group. Though no church will do all of these things, every congregation can do something wonderful. Pastors who are loved work harder, stay longer and feel more secure than those who are held at arm's length by lay leaders.

Today, show your pastor and family that they are loved in tangible ways. Besides being a wonderful thing to do, an act of kindness will positively revolutionize the atmosphere of your church. It is a gift you give your pastor, but it is also a gift of new motivation that you and your church will receive from your pastor.

A little praise goes a long way. Affirming, appreciating and admiring your pastors are the best ways to help them enjoy ministry for a lifetime and bring out the best initiative and loyal service from these men and women of God.

INTANGIBLE GIFTS EVERY PASTOR NEEDS

Ministers cherish visible signs of love, and because of the message they communicate to pastors and their families, the giving of those gifts needs to increase. A fresh awareness of the need for clergy affirmation and appreciation appears to be growing across the land—and this is reason to rejoice. But an additional category of gifts is also needed. While these gifts cost no money, they represent high commitment levels by those who give them. These intangible gifts are highly significant, because they create wholesome relationships and stimulate a Christlike spirit in the church.

To enrich yourself and your own service to Christ, try giving one gift from this list to your pastor each week. You probably will no longer need the list after a few weeks, because giving these leadership gifts will have become spontaneous and habitual. Check the list to determine what your gifts will be.

Purity
Lay leaders must live clean lives. Live by the biblical admonition, "Among you there must not be even a hint of sexual immorality, or of any kind of impurity, or of greed, because these are improper for God's holy people" (Eph. 5:3).

Trust
Believe in your pastor with your whole heart. Overlook his faults. Build confidence for your pastor among your brothers and sisters in Christ. Refuse to listen to gossip or circulate suspicion.

Love
Unlike cheap love of the world, this gift is the love of the Lord. It is an unconditional, volitional love that wants the highest and best for another. The pattern for this love can be found in the apostle Paul's powerful charge, "Be imitators of God, therefore, as dearly loved children and live a life of love, just as Christ loved us and gave himself up for us as a fragrant offering and sacrifice to God" (Eph. 5:1-2). Esteem and affection between laypersons and their pastor are absolutely essential for doing ministry that pleases God.

Acceptance
Being accepted by a congregation is a critical requirement for doing effective ministry. Sometimes a new minister is not accepted quickly enough, because the congregation is still grieving the loss of a former leader. But since everyone plans to accept the new pastor sooner or later, why not sooner?

Followership
No one can effectively lead who does not follow. David McKenna's

book title summarizes the issue: *Power to Follow and Grace to Lead.*
Assure your pastor that you want to follow and that you are eager
for her to lead your church. Chaos and bedlam result when a
church lacks a faithful followership.

Christ-Centeredness

From beginning to end, the church is about Jesus. He is the foundation and cornerstone. Without Christ at the center, the church
becomes a human institution that does good things, but it is not
the church. Encourage your minister by sharing your spiritual-
growth experiences with him. The spiritual development of the
congregation is among a pastor's most significant sources of
encouragement and reflects his effectiveness in the ministry.

Faithfulness

Every pastor needs your faithful attendance, generous giving
and wholehearted loyalty. Such faithfulness is the foundation of
all that is done in the local church. God's faithfulness is our
model.

Fairness

Integrity, kindness, fairness and magnanimity all make the work
of the church move ahead smoothly. When your sense of fair
play is tested, ask yourself, "What would Jesus do?" Then do it.

Unity

No one should expect 100 percent agreement in the church on
every issue. But every church needs leaders who help create a
bond of ministry that produces unity. Too much talk about differences always clouds the issues. Every church has persons who
undermine unity, who should not be chosen as church leaders
because the pressures are too great and their predictable
responses are too destructive.

This list of intangible gifts could be expanded. You might add concepts like forgiveness, friendship, humanity, grace, humility and benefit of the doubt. But an important point has been made—some of the most valuable gifts lay leaders can give their pastor or themselves is to be authentically Christian both inside and outside the church.

RENEWAL STRATEGIES FOR LAY LEADERS: SHOWING YOUR PASTOR LOVE

1. Be sure your love impacts every phase of a pastor's ministry.
2. Realize that affirming is something anyone can do.
3. Start a whole church campaign to show your pastor how important he is.
4. Undermine suspicion and criticism with appreciation.
5. Praise, especially during tough times.
6. Report secondhand compliments and see the amazing motivating power it generates.
7. Create memories for your pastor and enrich everyone involved in the process.
8. Speak up. Quiet or unexpressed appreciation makes no impact.
9. Plan appreciation events. Some people will take part in such an event who would not otherwise express their gratitude.
10. Write your affirmation down. Something special happens when your pastor receives a written word of encouragement or praise.

Notes

1. Janis Allen, quoted in Bob Nelson, *1001 Ways to Reward Employees* (New York: Workman Publishing, 1994), p. 30.
2. Richard File, ibid., p. 10.

ARE WE UP FOR THE CHALLENGE?

The church of Jesus Christ worldwide is facing a crisis of identity and decreasing influence. At times it appears that we are simply treading water; yet the awesome responsibility of the Church has not changed—we are to impact our world with the loving, life-changing message of Jesus Christ. It is a message every dedicated layman and committed pastor must heed. Are we doing our best?

As we (Neil and H. B.) travel this country, we see the Church grasping for nearly anything that works, while in nation after nation the world is being led to salvation one person at a time by an army of laymen who still feel that the salvation of mankind is their responsibility.

We are observers of the Church in America. Statistics say that in spite of all the seeker-sensitive methods used to reach the lost, fewer non-Christians are coming to church. Churches are not simply about filling seats; they are about preaching and teaching a message of repentance. Yet thousands of churches will not see one person come to know Christ this year. Why? Because they have lost a vision for the unsaved.

When asked, "What is the greatest challenge you face as a pastor?" ministers in our survey responded, "The apathy of laymen. Our people have very little passion for the message of the Great Commission." Well, folks, we had better generate some passion, or the world will continue to be unsaved and unimpressed by our "Madison Avenue" approach. Unbelievers are looking for something genuine, not just something that glitters. So what can we do?

PRAY for a revival in your own life. The prayer of David is a good place to begin. "Search me, O God, and know my heart; test me and know my anxious thoughts. See if there is any offensive way in me, and lead me in the way everlasting" (Ps. 139:23-24).

PRAY that God will burden your heart for the unsaved.

PRAY that God will place you in a field of spiritual harvest.

PRAY that your pastor and church leaders will have courage to preach and speak the Word of God with boldness and work together in unity and harmony.

It is not too late. There is a cloud on the horizon. The cloud is small, but it is filled with promise and looks like it might bring blessing and renewal to our land.

ADDITIONAL RESOURCES FOR PASTORS AND CHURCHES

PASTORAL RESOURCES AND SERVICES AVAILABLE FROM THE PASTORAL MINISTRIES DEPARTMENT OF FOCUS ON THE FAMILY

The resources listed in this section are available by calling 1-800-A-FAMILY or visiting www.parsonage.org.

Website

The Parsonage (www.parsonage.org)—a home page for ministers and their families.

Toll-free Phone Line

The Pastoral Care Line (1-877-233-4455)—a listening ear or word of advice from our staff of pastors for ministers, missionaries, chaplains and their families.

Audiocassettes

Pastor to Pastor—an audiocassette series available as a bimonthly subscription or individual sets. Features H. B. London interviewing Christian experts on topics pertaining to the personal and family lives of pastors, such as pastors in crisis, keeping romance alive, overcoming weariness, retaining your own identity as a pastor's wife, dangers of the Internet and pastors as parents.

Newsletter

The Pastor's Weekly Briefing—a quick look at current events of interest to pastors, their families and their congregations. Available by fax or e-mail or at the website.

Congregational Booklets

The Pastor's Advocate Series—a set of booklets designed to help congregations better understand pastors and their families, better care for them and better join them in ministry.

Resource Directory

The Pastoral Care Directory—an invaluable list of ministries specializing in care for pastoral families, plus the best in books, audiocassettes, videos, publications and other resources (available both in print and online).

BOOKS AVAILABLE FROM FOCUS ON THE FAMILY

London, Jr., H. B. *Refresh, Renew, Revive: How to Encourage Your Spirit, Strengthen Your Family, and Energize Your Ministry.* Colorado Springs, CO: Focus on the Family, 1996.

London, Jr., H. B., and Toler, Stan. *The Minister's Little Devotional Book.* Tulsa, OK: Honor Books, 1997.

London, Jr., H. B., and Wiseman, Neil B. *The Heart of a Great Pastor: How to Grow Strong and Thrive Wherever God Has Planted You.* Ventura, CA: Regal Books, 1994.

———. *Married to a Pastor: How to Stay Happily Married in the Ministry.* Ventura, CA: Regal Books, 1999.

———. *They Call Me Pastor: How to Love the Ones You Lead.* Ventura, CA: Regal Books, 2000.

BOOKS AVAILABLE AT AMAZON

Questions about these books and their availability can be directed to NBWBooks@aol.com.

Wiseman, Neil B. *Come to the Water Brook.* Kansas City, MO: Beacon Hill Press, 1997.
———. *Conditioning Your Soul.* Kansas City, MO: Beacon Hill Press, 1999.
———. *Hunger for the Holy—71 Ways to Get Closer to God.* Grand Rapids, MI: Baker Books, 1996.
———. *Maximizing Your Church's Spiritual Potential.* Kansas City, MO: Beacon Hill Press, 1999.
———. *The Untamed God—Unleashing the Supernatural in the Body of Christ.* Kansas City, MO: Beacon Hill Press, 1996.

PASTOR CONFERENCES AND SEMINARS

H. B. London and Neil B. Wiseman are available to speak at conferences, conventions and organizations concerning the ideas described in this book, pastoral renewal, the inner life of the Christian and the renewal of the supernatural in the Body of Christ. Wiseman, who has led the Small Church Institute since 1991, also does consulting with denominational leaders concerning issues facing smaller congregations.

INTERNET CONTACT INFORMATION

H. B. London: http://www.parsonage.org
Neil B. Wiseman: nbwiseman@aol.com